GW01158634

Migizi

Baron Alexander
& Lucky Deschauer

Dedicated to
Tommy Prince

Contents

First Day of School

He was the first boy I met when I arrived. He had red hair and skin that was lighter than mine. He smiled a lot. I knew I would like him when he told me his name.

"Geezis. You know, like Jesus, just different." He smiled and ran to the edge of the school building, peeked around the corner, and then looked back at me. I ran to join him.

"How long you been here?"

"A year, maybe longer."

"What are you doing?"

"Looking for the shadow."

I looked where he was staring and could only see the grass blowing in the autumn wind.

"You see it?"

"Yeah," I lied. I moved my head to the left and then the right to get a better view.

"It keeps moving. I track it."

"Have you ever caught it?"

"Not yet. Sometimes, it comes close. I can almost feel it. Then it disappears." He stopped looking and walked back to where we just were. I followed. His hair wasn't cut like mine. It was long, past his shoulders. I liked the way the sun danced in it.

I saw a bush and ran to it. "Come here. Look. Blueberries!" I started picking but stopped when he didn't join me. "What's up?"

He didn't answer. I returned to him and we played a game that he liked. It involved sticks and a little ball.

"Do you like?" he asked.

"It's OK. My uncle and father played something like it but they threw the ball with the stick."

"You've seen it?"

I felt important and shrugged. "Of course. Everyone plays."

He kicked the dirt and didn't say anything.

"Does the school have the proper ones?" I asked.

He shook his head. "They don't give us those things. I made this."

I looked at it again with renewed respect. "I think I like yours better."

He looked up and smiled. His whole face beamed. "Thanks."

Before I could pick up the stick to play, the school bell rang and we dropped everything and ran. A big woman covered in grey stood on the steps as we all ran towards the school. One look from her got my fellow classmates to stop running and form two lines. The girls formed a line and the boys another line. As this was my first day there, I got in behind Geezis. Everyone became silent and walked up the stairs. I could smell the nun as I passed her. She had a different smell than my mother and nothing like us students. Her face wasn't smiling.

I followed Geezis to the third classroom on the left. He sat in the back, nearest to the window. I sat in the desk next to him.

"Settle down, class. That's it." When everyone had found a seat, she continued. "Today, we have a new student."

All eyes turned and found me. Some smiled, most just stared. I didn't know why they were looking at me. I didn't understand her words.

"Stand up. Yes, you. Good." She pointed at me and I realized I didn't have an option. I stood up. "Tell us your name."

I stared at her.

"Your name," she repeated. Then, she pointed at herself. "Sister Agatha." Then she pointed at me.

"Migizi," I said. The other students laughed.

"Quiet down. I won't tolerate outbursts in my classroom." She glared at the offending students and I began to feel better. I liked that she stood up for me. "Come here," she said to me and waved at me to come forward and pointed with her finger to the spot next to her.

I shuffled towards the front of the class. I could feel every muscle and bone in my body. I could feel their eyes on me. I tried to think what I should say but my mind went blank. All I could see was her getting bigger as I got closer to her.

"As you are new here, I think you should introduce yourself to the class. I will start. My name is Sister Agatha. I will be your teacher this year." She smiled and then indicated it was my turn.

"My name is Migizi," I said, hoping I was using her words the right way. There was a little laughter, but not like before. I felt myself shaking and couldn't speak. I held up eight fingers. I don't know why they laughed at that.

"Very good, Mi–" Sister Agatha said. "But I think we're going to have trouble saying your name. How about, from now on, we call you David? Would you like that?"

I was shaking a lot and just wanted to return to my desk. I nodded because it seemed that's what I was supposed to do. I had no idea what she was saying.

"Good boy. OK, David, you can sit down. Everyone welcome David to our school." As I walked back, she began to clap and everyone else joined in. I was feeling hot and my palms were sweating by the time I got back to my desk.

"Now, today we are going to review what we learned yesterday. Open up your desks and pull out your notebook."

I didn't have anything in my desk. I looked to Geezis and he didn't either. The woman didn't take any notice and kept on talking. I raised my hand.

"Yes?"

I held out my two empty hands.

She paused and then went to a cupboard on the wall and took out a blue notebook. She seemed to notice something as she took out a second notebook. She then took out two pencils and placed them on her desk at the front of the room. She nodded towards the pile and then at me. I figured I needed to pick them up.

When I returned to my desk, I gave one notebook and one pencil to Geezis and kept one of each for

5

myself. I reached into my pocket and gave him a handful of blueberries I had picked earlier. He smiled at me and I knew I had made a new friend.

⁑

"Are we supposed to eat this?" I asked when lunch was served. The rest of the morning had been uneventful. Sister Agatha talked at us and I tried to understand what she was saying. I sat in the back, so she didn't see me. I wasn't called. I was happy when the lunch bell sounded.

"Just wait," he said.

"I'm starving," I said. I put my spoon in and tried it. "Eww! This is *awful!*"

"Shhh. Just eat it." Geezis waited with his hands in his lap. I didn't understand why he didn't try it. It was disgusting but it was still lunch.

"David!" The voice was loud. There were three teachers in the room now, all dressed in the same funny grey with something over their heads. The voice sounded like Sister Agatha. I guessed she was angry at one of the boys.

I took another bite.

"David!" The voice was right next to me. I turned around and saw my teacher standing there, face becoming reddish. I looked around to see who she was yelling at.

"Sister Agatha?" I said with a small voice.

In response, she grabbed my ear and made me stand up. She then led me to the front of the room where the other teachers were standing. I could see the eyes of the entire school on me. I didn't know what I had done wrong.

"I thought you were a good boy," she said, loud enough for the entire room to hear.

I began to shrink. I wasn't sure if I was supposed to answer.

"I guess I was wrong. Are you a bad boy?"

I couldn't say anything. I had begun to shake. All those eyes burned on me. And I had never had a strange elder yell at me before. If I had done something wrong, my mother or father would deal with me in private. She was still holding my ear and it hurt like nothing I had felt before.

"You know what we do to bad boys? We discipline them." She nodded to one of the other teachers who took a long wooden ruler off the blackboard on the wall. I noticed that this room wasn't just for eating. It was for teaching as well. It was like a very big classroom.

"Put your hands on the desk over there." She pointed to the large wooden teacher's desk as she directed me there by my ear. She let go and I put my

7

hand to my ear. "I said, hands on the table." The voice cut through the room and it became more silent than if there had been no people in it.

I put my hands flat on the table, fingers together. I didn't see the other teacher until I felt the pain. She slammed the yardstick on my fingers. I could see it raised to strike again but I had taken my hands away. My fingers were in my mouth and I could feel the tears begin to swell.

"You are turning out to be a very different boy than what I had hoped. Hands on the desk. *Now!*" She grabbed my other ear and I didn't know where the pain was coming from anymore. My hands hurt and, now, both my ears hurt. I did what she said and felt the wood hit my hands again. I began to cry.

"That's enough, Sister Christina," Sister Agatha said. The other teacher nodded and returned the yardstick to the blackboard. Sister Agatha turned to me and asked, "Are you going to be a good boy?"

I didn't know what she was saying but I nodded. Agreeing with her seemed the right thing to do.

"Then go back to your seat."

I did.

She waited until I was back in my seat and then she began to pray. All the other students bowed their heads and repeated what she said. I didn't know the prayer so I bowed my head and let the tears run slowly down my cheeks. I wasn't hungry anymore.

I heard Geezis say something to me after the heads were up and eyes opened. I couldn't understand what he said either. My head was swimming in anger, confusion, and shame for what had just happened.

"What?" I asked. It came out a little too loud and the students from the next table turned their heads. Geezis waited until their heads returned to their food before repeating himself.

"Your name."

"What about it?"

"You didn't respond to it."

"They never said my name."

"Your new name."

"I don't remember what she said."

"David."

"Oh," I said.

"Remember. It's hardest the first few days. Keep listening for it."

"OK."

"And the food."

"What about it?"

"Never eat it before grace."

*
*

I deserved it. I know that now. I just didn't know the rules. I told myself I wouldn't break any more of the school rules. I was always a good boy before I arrived here. My parents told me that every day.

We had to pray after our meal and then form two lines to go and work outside.

"Just do what I do," Geezis said.

"OK." I followed him outside.

"Watch out for the fat one. The one with the red face. She uses the strap faster than anyone."

I scanned the teachers and found the nun he was talking about. She wasn't shorter than any of the others, just fatter. I could see her laughing with one of the other nuns. "Why do they wear those strange clothes?" I asked.

"Those? I don't know. The sisters and Mother Superior wear funny clothes. Some of the brothers, too. But the outside teachers are better."

"How can you tell?"

"You'll see."

"Who's that guy?"

"He's Father O'Flaherty."

"He's also dressed funny."

"I know. But never say anything or it'll mean the strap."

I tried to understand. When I arrived, before I met my friend Geezis, I had to give all my clothes and belongings to one of the brothers. They said I'd get them back when I left. They gave me new clothes. I didn't mind. I looked like everyone else now.

"How come they didn't shave *your* head?" I asked. I was still getting used to having hair that showed my scalp. I noticed all the other kids had the same type of cut—except Geezis.

"I don't know," he said. "The Father specifically told them not to cut my hair."

I wanted to touch his hair. I'd never seen a boy with long red hair before. No one else in the school had red hair, not even the girls. He didn't seem to mind and began to run towards the garden.

"Why are we running? They're just going to make us work."

He turned and looked at me and smiled again. His hair covered his face as he did so. "We want to get the best job."

"What is the best job?"

"One where we can eat while we pick." He sped up and we got to the edge of the garden at the same time as the older boys. They looked to be either ten or twelve.

"This is our area, Jesus." He was four inches taller than Geezis and three more of his friends arrived by the time I got there. "You can deal with the potatoes."

"Why don't you dig for potatoes?" Geezis said. I stood behind him the way the other boy's three friends stood behind him.

The taller boy stepped forward and pushed Geezis. "Go play with yourself. We're doing the corn and the carrots."

Geezis launched himself head first at the older boy. All I saw was the flurry of red hair and his feet pushing. The older boy was surprised and fell over. Even some of his friends stumbled.

"You can stick your potatoes," he screamed. He then jumped on the boy and began punching his head. I still don't know whether it was from shock or fear that the older boy didn't fight back. I tried to look tough in order to keep the other three boys away, but two men rushed between us. They picked up Geezis and told me to join him. The other man grabbed the older boy. I found out later that these two men were called brothers Georges and Nicholas.

"What is this about?" The darker brother Georges said when he had pulled us apart.

"Ogimaa won't let us pick the corn. Or the carrots. And we got here first today." Geezis' face was smeared with mud and his nose was bleeding. Other than that, he looked fired up. I stood taller with pride.

"Who?" Brother Georges had his hand on the strap.

"Matthew," Geezis said, suddenly aware of who he was talking to.

Brother Georges swung and hit him on his bare leg with the strap. He hit again. No tears. He then hit the other leg. I saw Geezis grimace but held back the tears. "The first two were for the fighting. The third was for refusing to call your classmate by his name."

I got one strap for participating and felt pretty good. I deserved something but at least it wasn't three. I don't think I could have handled it as well as Geezis.

"Joseph."

"What?" I heard the name but didn't know what he was talking about.

"You're supposed to call me Joseph and not Jesus. If you call me Geezis, you'll get the strap." He walked back to where the potatoes were and we took the little shovel and began to dig.

"Careful not to cut the potatoes. You need to loosen the dirt next to the dead plants, then you get on your knees and feel for the potatoes."

"OK," I said. I didn't comment on the names, but I saw what happened when the rules were broken.

"Just put the potatoes next to where you have dug. We'll come back later and pick them up."

"How did you learn so much about this?"

"Last year."

"You learned a lot. I've never seen a potato except on a plate."

Geezis liked that. "Nothing to it." His leg was showing a big red welt where the strap hit him in the same spot. Mine wasn't so bad. The bigger boys were stripping the corn and digging up carrots. I could see them sneaking some of the food into their pockets.

"They're taking food for later."

"Don't snitch," he said.

"Why not? They'd do it to us. Besides, I don't want to break the rules."

"The teachers have their rules and we have ours. Don't snitch."

I wanted to say something. It didn't seem fair. I kept my head down and put the shovel into the ground and pulled on the handle. The ground became loose and I did it all over again. By the time the bell rang, we had done the entire row. We were filthy from the dirt but happy. I enjoyed it.

On the way back to the main building, Brother Nicholas pulled me aside.

"You can't go back like that. You're too dirty." He had me by the shoulder.

"I can clean up inside," I said.

"Let me. We should be able to knock that dirt off you." He began dusting and patting me to drive off all the dirt. It worked. My T-shirt looked almost clean and my jeans were normal, except for some grass stains on my knees that wouldn't come out from that technique.

"Thanks!"

"Hurry up. You don't want to be late." He smiled and waved me back into the line.

Geezis had saved me a seat next to him for supper. We kneeled first as Father O'Flaherty said the prayers. He left us to the nuns and we all sat down. There were a lot of us there, all the girls and boys and all the grades. I was with the younger students as I was in Grade Three. The older boys sat together by grade. The girls were on one half of the room and we were on the other.

"I'm starving more than at lunch."

"Don't hold your breath."

"I don't care what it is. I'll love it." I was serious. I never came across a meal I couldn't eat.

Geezis looked at me with his elbows on the table. We watched as the older kids got their food and returned to their seats. It was done by the table. We were last. I hoped there would be food for us by the time we got there.

"It's not so bad," I said as I sat down.

"Looks like yesterday's and tomorrow's and all last year's," Geezis said.

I took a bite. "Not bad. Meat and potatoes. I wonder if they used the potatoes we just dug up."

"Really?"

I wasn't sure what I was supposed to say to that. I ate in silence for the rest of the meal. There wasn't any dessert. Sister Agatha led the prayers, while we knelt, after eating. We were then dismissed. We lined up two by two, as we did all day, and walked to our dorms. It wasn't far. We slept one floor up from the kitchen and dining room. The older boys and girls slept in separate dorms upstairs. The school was separate from where we ate and slept. I was happy about that for some reason.

"Can I sleep next to you?" I asked Geezis.

"Sure. Grab a bed and make sure everyone knows it's yours. You should be OK."

I looked at the single bed on the steel frame. "Don't we get any covers?"

"In winter, yes. I'm hoping they'll give us some blankets now as well."

"Don't you get cold?"

"You get used to it."

"Being cold?"

He smiled. I was starting to become afraid. It was the first time that I missed my home and my parents. I've been cold before, but I always had my parents to warm me up. And we had blankets. And a fire on very cold days. I could feel the concrete on my feet and the cold rising up into me.

"Everyone, time for prayers. On your knees. Good. Take your rosary out and recite the Apostles' Creed and The Lord's Prayer with me." Brother Nicholas had come into our room and cast his eye over all the beds. His eyes fell on me briefly. I nodded. He smiled in return. I didn't know what a rosary was or what they wanted to pray about. I decided to keep my mouth shut, kneel and hope no one noticed.

The concrete was colder on my knees than my bare feet. It hurt but I knew I had to stay down. I looked around and everyone was on their knees. They were all saying the prayer out loud. I felt ashamed that I was the only one stupid enough not to know it. I was determined to stay on my knees but it hurt. I looked at Brother Nicholas and noticed him looking at me. He must have known that I didn't know the words.

"Back in bed. Lights out."

He left without doing anything to me. I felt the relief as I sunk into my bed. I thought about the look on my parents' faces when I left for school. I had never seen my dad cry before and he had just returned a hero from the war. I even saw the medal. But his eyes were brimming earlier today. My mother looked at me like her face was set in stone. I didn't understand what they were concerned about. School seemed fine to me.

CHAPTER TWO

Speak Only English

"The shadow is back."

I looked to see what he was talking about.

"It rolls along the edge of the field, see?"

I didn't see.

"Last year the shadow came *this close*." He held his fingers a couple of inches apart.

I didn't want to tell Geezis I couldn't see anything. I didn't understand, but he knew the school. I thought I'd wait. Maybe I'd see the shadow eventually. Besides, he had been in school for a year. I had only been going for a day.

"Swings?" He turned away from the same corner as the day before and ran towards the swings. They were usually full but we found one swing to share.

I watched him tuck his legs behind him as he went backwards and make them straight as he came down and up. His hair looked like fire in the morning sun. I wished I was more like him.

Earlier that morning wasn't easy. The brothers came in clapping for us to get up, pray, shower, and eat. We were now enjoying the few minutes before we had to go to the other building. I liked the dorm better than the school. At least I could learn the rules. School was something I wasn't sure I would be good at.

I got two turns on the swing before the bell went and we had to go to the classroom. I noticed Father O'Flaherty watching over the schoolyard from the steps of the school. I thought he was looking at us. By the time we got to the school, he had returned inside. I noticed Sister Agatha standing where the Father had been and she ensured we all got back to our classes.

"Settle down, class. Good. Today we will be practicing writing. I have written something on the board. Can anyone read it for me? You, Timothy, stand up."

She pointed to a boy in the class I didn't know yet. His face looked dirty, like he forgot to wash. His hair had been cut short, like mine. He wore almost identical jeans to me, with the front going all the way up the chest and back with clasps that held it together. He had a red shirt on. Mine was blue.

He stood without speaking, his eyes lowered.

"Timothy? Anything wrong?"

He said nothing. His face seemed to get dirtier as he stood there.

She let him stand and turned to us. "Class, this is an example of what you do not want to be. You need to be reading and writing by now. Is there anyone who can read this? David?"

I shook my head. I could barely understand the English she spoke. I heard her speaking some other language to the other nuns.

"Joseph?"

My friend stood up and looked intently at the board. "*Je ne comprends pas*," he said. I turned and looked at him as though he had spoken alien. I then turned to look at Sister Agatha's face. I thought I saw a hint of a smile.

"*Assieds-toi, mon fils*," she said. "You, too, Timothy. Sit down." She returned to the board in front of the class. "OK. So we need to go back to the basics. You will write out the alphabet in small and capital letters. We will then begin to put those letters together to form words. Can anyone tell me what a word is?"

A girl in the front raised her hand. I noticed her hair wasn't cut as short as mine.

"Everything is a word," she said.

"Correct," smiled the sister. "We take letters and they create words. Words are what we speak when we talk to each other. We write them down so we can communicate with others—in books or letters." She began to erase what she had written on the board and replaced it with the alphabet. There was nothing else in the room showing us how the letters looked.

The rest of the morning was spent doing that. I had seen my parents draw and write. They were respected in my community. When my dad joined the army, my mom would sing to me and we would play games. But, I don't remember learning the alphabet. It was strange. Almost as weird as the strange language Geezis spoke—or that the sister replied in. I felt even more stupid that morning.

Lunch was exactly as the day before. Some soup with swollen bread floating on the top. We had a glass of milk because the men who were supposed to pick it up didn't come. The cows produced milk whether they came or not. I was told getting milk was a treat and we should enjoy it. I did.

The afternoon wasn't as fun as yesterday because we didn't get to the garden in time. We were forced to gather the dead plants and hay. I don't know if they fed it to the cows or horses or burned it. I just collected it. The only thing I enjoyed was being next to Geezis.

"What language did you speak in class?" I asked.

"French."

"You speak French?"

"And Ojibwe. My mother is Ojibwe and my father was French."

I looked with renewed respect at my friend. Each time I learned something more about him, he seemed smarter and better than I had expected. "Did you father go to war as well?"

He lowered his head. "He died this summer. I heard just before I came back to school."

I didn't know what to say. He was the only person I knew whose father had died.

"And I speak English."

I laughed. "I know. We're speaking it now."

He laughed. "Sometimes I don't know. I like speaking French but there is no one to speak it with other than my family." He didn't say anything about the Indian language he spoke. I didn't either.

We scratched the ground some more with our rakes before I continued. "What are you going to do without a dad?"

"I don't know." He started looking at the edge of the field like he did earlier. I couldn't see what he was looking at.

"Are you now the head of your family?"

"I don't know. I'm the oldest kid but my uncle and grandparents do most of the things that need to be done."

"I have a grandmother who makes medicine," I said. "She makes me go with her into the bush. I carry what she picks. Sometimes, she uses a knife and takes some of the bark off trees. Sometimes, she gathers grass or even branches of the tree. She gives it to me and we go back home. Then, she does something with it and it becomes medicine. Everyone says she is the best healer we could have."

"We have someone like that, but he's a man—"

Our conversation was interrupted with the sound of leather hitting skin. I realized it was my skin and began to cry. It was a delayed reaction. I didn't realize I was hurt until I saw the brother standing over me with an angry face. I think it was the face I was crying at more than the hit. He also hit Geezis but he didn't cry.

"You know the rules. No talking about those things," he said.

"What are you—?" I tried to ask him what I had done wrong. Instead of a reply, I got another hit by the strap. I shut up after that.

"You are to speak only English in this school. You are not to bring your heathen ways into this place." His face was getting red as he leaned over us. "Do you understand?"

"Yes," I said.

"*Oui,*" Geezis said. Then he quickly corrected himself. "Yes."

The brother glared at my friend and then me. Then he walked away. Everyone stopped to watch us being disciplined. I wanted the ground to open up and swallow me but it didn't. It stood firm and held me. I felt the soil between my fingers. It felt good.

"Is that what Sister Agatha speaks?"

"French. Yes."

"Is that why she likes you?"

"I don't think she likes me," he said. He started scratching the ground again with his rake. I didn't ask any more questions. I didn't want the brother to come back.

We weren't allowed to stop working until almost five o'clock. It was that time of year. There was a clock in the dorm and I was taught by my mother how to read the clock when I was young. I noticed the other boys and most of the girls didn't know how to read the clock yet. I just wanted to eat and go to sleep.

Dinner was the same as the night before. Boiled meat and potatoes. I started eating and was finished before I knew it. I wanted seconds but the food was already all gone.

We still had prayers and I didn't like kneeling on the concrete. I did my best and didn't draw any attention to myself. There were extra prayers for the sick kids who couldn't come to class or work in the fields. I had heard them coughing but didn't think much of it. We all coughed once in a while. Geezis told me that some were so sick they had to lay in bed all day. I wished that I could be sick so I didn't have to go to class or work outside all afternoon.

We went to bed and I was pleased that they had brought covers. It wasn't cold but it was hard to sleep without covers. I turned to say goodnight to Geezis but noticed he was gone. I thought he must be using the toilet. I turned the other way and closed my eyes. I slept a deep sleep, content with the sounds of all the other boys sleeping in the same room as me.

CHAPTER THREE

No Hunting Allowed

I learned the rules of the dorm and the school fairly quickly. They made it easy for us by making sure every day was the same—except for Sunday. Every day, we cleaned ourselves, prayed, ate and went to class. Every day we ate the same mush for breakfast. The only variation was that sometimes it was harder than others. I think they must have made it the night before because it was always cold. We would get milk with it. I liked it. Geezis said that sometimes they served sour milk, but I had only been there two weeks and I never noticed that.

Every lunch was the same. It was some type of soup. I couldn't tell what was in it or what floated on it from time to time. It was disgusting but I ate it. I always ate everything at home and it would be wasteful not to eat it. The other boys complained a lot. I heard them grumble. I even heard that the older boys would raid the kitchen to find food after everyone had gone to sleep. That was all talk as far as I was concerned. I made sure I was next to Geezis at all times. He knew what needed to be done and how to get it done. I was glad he was my friend.

Then dinner would come along and it was the same as always. In two weeks, I noticed that sometimes my portions of meat were bigger or smaller. It didn't make any sense but I ate what I was given. I didn't want to get the strap or a scolding in front of the other students.

Sunday meant we had to spend more time in the showers and wear our cleanest clothes. The water was cold and I didn't like it. I didn't think I was dirty to begin with. But the brothers made sure we all showered. One of the boys resisted and the older boys had to hold him under the shower until he crumpled to the floor in tears. The older boys looked to the brothers to see what they were supposed to do. They left the boy to cry, alone.

The first Sunday Mass was hard to understand. They spoke in Latin. I didn't understand why we couldn't speak our language but they could speak French and Latin as much as they wanted. And they didn't teach us what any of it meant. I saw one of the girls receive a strap for giggling and telling jokes during the time they were supposed to be repeating what the priest said. The nuns were in the back of the chapel but someone must have told them. The girls got a beating from the fat nun with the red face. They said she enjoyed hitting the girls. All I know is that I never saw those girls giggle again during mass.

I sat next to my friend everywhere we went. On Sunday, I noticed something different about him. He sat staring at Father O'Flaherty as though he was a ghost. I didn't say anything but I wanted to shake him to make him wake up. It was as though he was sleeping with his eyes open.

When we were able to change, we raced to the swings. We each got one.

"I bet you can't go higher than me," I said.

"I bet you can't go all the way around," he said.

"Over the top?"

"Yeah," he smiled. "I keep looking at it and I'm sure we can do it. We just need more speed."

I decided to stand on the swing's seat. I then began to pull and push with my hands on the chains to get the swing to go higher. If it was possible, I would make it go around and over the top.

"Good idea." Geezis smiled and also stood up. We swung higher than any kid had swung before.

"Whoa," I said. "Did you see that?"

"No. What happened?"

"I got so high, the chain went loose. I was flying and then it snapped back. Didn't you see?"

"No. Try it again."

I did. I went higher and higher until the chain went loose. I could feel myself falling for the briefest of seconds. I was no longer connected to the chain or the swing or anything. Then it snapped back into place and I felt the wild movement of the chains as I was forced to swing back. I didn't make it over the top, but it was as high as I think you can go before going over the top.

"I saw it. Watch me!" He went higher and higher and the swing went limp as it went past the point of the usual path. When it pulled him back, he slipped off the swing. I saw it in slow motion. His left foot slipped off the back of the swing and his right slipped off the front. His body was held stationary in the air when the swing went backwards, pulling his one leg with it and causing his body to flip him downwards. He tumbled out of the air, face first, and landed in a heap on the ground.

I slowed down and then jumped off. I congratulated myself on being able to stay on but began to worry for Geezis when he wasn't moving.

"Geezis!"

Nothing.

I shook him and turned him over. His eyes were closed. I couldn't tell if he was breathing or not.

"Wake up!" I began screaming but no one came. The brothers and sisters were inside and most of the other kids were in the play area in the basement of the dorms. They associated the outside with work. The other kids looked my way but were too far away to see what happened. They probably thought I was playing a game. They ignored me.

I shook him some more and tried to straighten him out. *I've killed him*, I thought. I began to cry and held his head in my lap.

"Boo!" The voice caused me to jump and his head bounced out of my lap. Then I heard laughter and I looked around to see who would do something like that. When I looked down, I figured it out.

"You're OK!" I was so relieved. "I thought you were dead."

"Me, too! When I hit, the shadow came and touched me. Then I knew I would be OK."

"Are you hurt?"

In reply, he moved his arms, then legs, then head. "No."

"Do want to swing some more?"

He smiled at me. It was like the sun coming out from behind the clouds. "Not right away. Can we do something else?"

"How about berry picking?"

"I don't know how."

"I'll show you." I was even prouder that I knew something he didn't. It was something I did every season with my grandmother and mother. They would make jelly and preserve them for the winter. We needed to watch out for bears. When they came, we left.

It was late for berries, but we found some blueberries and blackberries. "Usually, the birds get these," I said.

"Hmmm." He had a mouthful and couldn't talk. I could see the black juice from the berries trickle out of his mouth. He looked happy.

"Do you think we would be allowed to hunt some of the rabbits?"

He swallowed and then became serious. "They won't allow you. They don't want you to do anything other than the stuff they do. Read, write, go to church, and wear funny clothes. That's all I think they want us to do. Can you imagine them letting you make arrows and start hunting?"

I looked at him with a blank face. "Yes. Why not? They don't seem to have enough food and we can help."

Geezis was silent and picked some more berries. "These are good."

I didn't say anything more about hunting. I wasn't any good. I just wanted to practice. I didn't have a bow but I could make some arrows. Not sure if I would get anything anyway.

Don't Ask, Don't Tell

I can't remember the exact date it happened. We woke just like any other day. We cleaned up, prayed, ate, and went outside before class began. Geezis was quieter than usual. He had a slight limp, like he was in pain. He didn't say anything about it. Instead, he peeked around the corner of the school and looked at the edge of the field.

"It's closer. I can see it much more clearly," he said. He had the same vacant look in his eye that I first saw in mass when he looked at Father O'Flaherty.

I still couldn't see what he was talking about. It was becoming annoying because it made me feel stupid. And I knew I wasn't stupid. The older boys were digging just beyond the playground, where the field began. Usually, I could hear the sounds of them talking or even yelling. Sometimes, I could hear them laughing at something. Today, they dug in silence.

I found out why later that morning. We were summoned to the edge of the field and I saw a hole where the boys were digging. I didn't go too close.

"What's happened?" I asked Geezis. He seemed to know everything and I never got the strap for asking him anything—unless I asked it and the adults heard.

"Another one."

"Another what?"

"The coughing. It kills them."

I had noticed a lot of us were coughing but that was normal. We'd get sick, then better. "Who is it?"

"Some girl two years older than us."

"I didn't know there was a sick girl here."

"She stayed in a special room where the nuns would pray over her."

"How do you know this?" I never understood how I knew so little compared to him.

"I've been—" He stopped and then looked embarrassed. "I've seen her before. I've seen the nuns praying."

I wondered what other secrets the school held. I knew it was big, but didn't know it could have a section with sick kids in it and I didn't know about it. I stayed quiet, standing at the edge of the field.

Soon, I saw the Father walking solemnly from the dormitory towards us. He was dressed in his Sunday clothes. Behind him were the brothers. They were carrying something. Behind it were the nuns.

The sun was shining bright and there was little wind. The fields had been cleared and we were waiting for winter to arrive. My mind drifted to how hard it must have been to dig the hole. I scanned the horizon for any rabbits that may be around. I noticed a handful of deer at the edge of my vision on the far side of the field. They must be eating the remains of the crop.

"Dear Heavenly Father, please accept this child of yours into your arms." The voice of Father O'Flaherty was strong and clear. I was startled by his voice as I preferred to watch the deer. Now, the girl had arrived. She was being carried on a stretcher and was wrapped in white sheets.

The Father continued talking for a while longer and the body was lowered into the hole. I wondered why she didn't have more protection from the animals. When he had finished talking, we were told to go to class. I noticed two of the older boys stayed behind. I saw them reach for the shovels as I rounded the school. They were out of sight after that.

"Why did they bury her there?" I asked Geezis.

"I don't know. They have buried a lot of kids there."

I stopped. "Is that why you look over there? Is that where the shadow comes from?"

"No. The shadow is my spirit. It protects me." He said it as though he was talking about something real—like the deer in the field or the rabbits I always looked for. I decided not to ask more about it right then.

I noticed the graveyard on our first day but just remembered it now. "Why didn't they bury her over there?" I pointed to the area that had a low metal fence around it with smooth slabs of stone. There was a small statue of a woman there as well.

"I don't know," he said. He also stopped and looked at where I pointed. "Maybe 'cause she's an Indian."

I wanted to ask, but I knew the answer. We weren't good enough to be buried in a proper way. I didn't see any gravestones where the girl was buried. Until the ceremony, I didn't even know it was a burial ground.

I followed behind his bouncing red hair. We were first into the building and went to class. I didn't know how I felt. I didn't know the girl. I didn't know she had died. I didn't know there was a burial ground. I don't know what I was supposed to do. So I sat next to Geezis by the window in the back of the class and watched Sister Agatha try to teach us the alphabet and numbers and words. She seemed to really care about it and I wanted to be a good boy so I listened. I learned. I managed to make it through my classes without being hit by the ruler or strap. I felt good about that. All I needed to do was exactly what they told me and I would be OK.

✳

The days turned into weeks. I learned what was expected of me. Weeks turned into months, and the snow began to fall. My family didn't live near enough for me to go home for Christmas holidays. Many of the students were in the same situation and had to stay at the dorm. I was looking forward to it.

"Your family isn't picking you up either?"

"No." Geezis didn't look at me.

"Want to try swinging and jump into the snow?"

There was a brief flicker, a hesitation, then the same response. "No."

"Do you want to make a snowman?"

"No."

"I bet I can beat you running around the school."

"Probably."

Then I knew something was wrong. Geezis was older and faster than me. Anything I can do, he could do better. I liked that he let me hang out with him. I let him stay in his bed and I decided to look around. Between the coughing and the holidays, almost half of the boys in my part were gone. I don't know about the older boys or the girls. I guess it must be the same.

Timothy started coughing shortly after the girl died and was buried. He slept on the other side of me. I don't talk to him much and he doesn't say anything. Then he began to cough and it didn't get better. One morning, he woke and saw blood on his pillow. He was so afraid of getting the strap, he turned it over and didn't tell the brother. It was only when he collapsed after lunch that he was taken to the part of the dorm where all the sick kids go. It was where the girl who died went. And that was where I was going now.

I don't know about other schools, but my school was big with lots of wood and stone and brick. My parents' place was made of wood only. The stairs were wide and swallowed up all the students, but even then there were times when it could have been bigger. The floors were all wood and we had to clean them every Saturday. The older boys did the windows because they had to climb on ladders. Each classroom had a single door that led into it with a window so that the adults could see in. I wasn't tall enough yet for that.

The hallways were long because it was the length of the entire building. The area I was looking for was on the other end. I was full of energy and didn't understand why Geezis was feeling so moody. The other kids had their own friends so I thought I'd go by myself.

"Hello, David."

"Uh, hello, Father."

"Are you looking for anything?"

"Uh, no, Father."

"Are you going anywhere?" He had come up to me and put his arm around my shoulder and walked in the same direction I was going.

"I wanted to see where all the sick kids were."

He stopped and turned me to look at him. "Why would you want to do that? Aren't you afraid you'll get sick?"

"You aren't afraid." I regretted it the moment the words left my mouth.

There was a look of surprise on his face, then it relaxed into a smile. The smile broadened and he started laughing. As he did, he pulled me close to him and patted me on the back. I could smell his clothing; it smelled a little rancid, as though it was decomposing on him. "You're a funny boy, David. I like that."

I felt my face redden.

"How would you like something special? Just for you."

I raised my eyes and then shoulders in a shrug.

"I have some candy in my office. Would you like some?"

I didn't want to tell him that I never tasted candy before. I nodded. "Yes, Father."

"Come with me. We'll take a peek at those poor children on our way." He held me close as we walked. His fingers moved on my shoulder, as though he was feeling the bone and muscle and imagining it in his mind.

We walked in silence. I tried not to think about his smell. When we got to the room with the kids, I was amazed at how many beds there were. I counted four beds by ten beds and each one was full. The room was full of natural sunshine and children of all ages, but mainly from my group.

"Satisfied? Or do you want to have a closer look?"

"That's OK, Father."

"Great. Let's go to my office." He let his hand move to my neck and I could feel his hand on my back. He was like a shepherd guiding his flock. I was his sheep, I guess.

His office had a door just like all the classrooms except there was no glass to see through. It smelled of smoke and I could smell something else but I didn't know what it was.

"Choose whatever you want." He took a bowl of candy from his desk drawer and put it in front of me. I didn't know what they were. They were red and white and yellow and green. I chose a red one and popped it into my mouth.

"Hmmm." I smiled as the first of the sugar was dissolved by my tongue and saliva. "Tank you." I didn't mean to speak incorrectly and the thought crossed my mind that I'd get the strap. I could see him moving his right arm but it landed softly on my head.

"You're welcome, David. Sit over there."

I did. He opened another drawer and pulled out a bottle with yellow liquid in it. He poured it into a glass and took a drink. It couldn't have been water because he didn't finish very much of it. I noticed it went back to his lips many times, each time taking a little sip. He came around from behind his desk and sat on the chair next to me.

"You like it?"

"Yes, Father." I made sure the candy was in my cheek before I talked this time.

"We need to keep this as our secret. You know how the other boys are. They won't understand."

I nodded. All the kids were jealous of anything. I noticed it but never put it into words the way Father O'Flaherty did. He was smart that way.

"Good boy." He patted my leg and then left his hand there. He took another drink.

"Father?"

"Yes, my son?"

"Can I have another piece?"

He laughed. "Of course you may. Help yourself."

I did and returned to my seat. I had two candies in my mouth. I never thought anything could taste so good.

Father O'Flaherty leaned back in his chair as he finished off his drink. "I think you should be going now, David. We'll meet again soon and you can have more candy. Would you like that?"

"Yes, Father." I got up and went to the door. I turned around as I put my hand on the door knob.

"Thank you, Father." He nodded and waved me out. I left and closed the door.

When I got back to my bed, Geezis was still in bed. I shook him.

"Get up," I said.

"I don't want to."

"I've got something for you."

He turned towards me. His eyes were usually like bright beacons when they opened; today they were shadows of their usual selves.

"Here." I spat out both candies. "Take the one you want."

He looked at my hand and the saliva that covered the candies and my skin. He also liked the red one and took it and popped it in his mouth. It made me feel good when I saw him smile.

"Thanks," he said.

"That's what friends are for."

"Want to swing into the snow?" He asked this time.

"I thought you'd never ask! Let's go!"

✲

I never saw a doctor in the dorm. The nuns would pray over the sick and it was up to God whether they were healed or not. I guess God wanted them back, because all of them died that Christmas. I was walking to Father O'Flaherty's office and noticed all the beds were empty. I don't know where they went. I didn't know any of them, except for Timothy. Father O'Flaherty held me tight when I asked him. He even gave me extra candy.

"Do you think Jesus took them?" I asked Geezis when I had returned.

"Maybe."

"Where could they have gone?"

"I don't know. Maybe shadow knows."

I never knew what to say when he talked about his shadow. "Maybe they got better and went home?"

"Probably," he said.

If Geezis didn't know, no one would know. I let the subject drop and sat on my bed next to where he was sitting. He didn't want to go out very often and spent most of his time curled up under his covers. Perhaps it was the view from our window. It was white as far as the eye could see. The school wasn't visible from where we looked out, nor were the cottages for the married teachers.

"Do you miss your mom?" I asked.

He looked up. "Yeah. But I don't like to think about it."

"Why?"

"'Cause she is there and we are here. If I could, I would run away and go back home."

"Really? Would you take me?"

"Of course. And anyone else who wants to come."

"I can make arrows. Can you make a bow?"

"Not really. The best bow-maker is my uncle. He would make them for the entire community."

"I can't wait until summer. I want to learn how to hunt."

"I can fish. It's easy. And you can do it in the winter."

Geezis knew everything. "Do you think they'll let us fish now?"

"No. They'll probably hit us for thinking like this."

"They don't want us to eat?"

"Only the mush they feed us."

"Maybe we can sneak some food? There must be some in the kitchen." I had heard that the older boys got away with it. There weren't as many teachers or nuns around now.

His smile gave me his answer. He swung his legs out from his covers and stood up. He winced when he walked. The kitchen was in the basement, one floor below us. All we had to do was avoid the adults. We walked barefoot to make less noise. We walked close to the wall to avoid creaking on the stairs. The concrete floor was especially cold on our feet and we began to run towards the kitchen. We could hear noises from the playroom next to the kitchen.

"It's open," I whispered. I pushed against the door and walked in. I had never been alone in the kitchen before. It was always full of bodies cooking, and serving. Now, it was clean with wide spaces between the worktops. We scanned the surfaces and walls to see where the food may be kept.

"Over here," Geezis said. He found a door that led to a room full of jars with stuff inside.

"Everything is pickled," I said.

"That's okay with me. Try this one." He pulled a jar from the shelf. It looked like chopped fish.

"That looks disgusting," I said.

"OK. Grab another. We'll try them both."

I grabbed some dill pickles. I liked the salty-sour taste.

"Let's get out of here," he said. "Back to our room. We can hide the jars somewhere."

I nodded and we hugged our treasure and returned to our beds. There was no one else in the room at this time of day. They were either outside playing or in the playrooms in the basement. He tried to open his first. It wasn't easy. Then, I held the

48

bottom glass and he gripped the top with both hands and used his entire body to turn it. The metal part eventually moved and we unscrewed it.

"We need a piece of metal like a knife or anything to break the seal." On the top of the jar was a piece of glass with a rubber seal. I thought it would come off when we unscrewed the metal lid. Again, Geezis knew what to do.

"Here." I handed him a file I shared with him to keep our nails trimmed. The brothers would give us the strap if we allowed our nails to grow too long.

He took it and slid it between the rubber and the glass. It sounded to me like a person inhaling quickly, then a pop as he turned his wrist while holding the file and the seal was broken. The room began to fill with the smell of fish.

"How're we going to eat it?"

"Fingers." He put his fingers into the jelly and found a piece of fish. He pulled it out and put it into his mouth. His eyes went to the side as though he was thinking about what was going on in his mouth. I waited to hear his verdict.

"And? How is it?"

He answered by putting his fingers in again. He was able to get his whole hand into the jar. He pulled out another piece and handed it to me. "Try it. It's good. Gooey, but good."

"Can't be worse than some of the stuff they feed us," I said. "I think there were worms in my boiled meat one time." I took the fish and put the whole thing into my mouth. It was hard to chew but I immediately liked the taste of the goo. It was like jelly my mother would put on my food for special occasions. I couldn't describe it at first. It was salty and sweet and a little sour all at once. Then I noticed the fish. Its flesh was more solid than the jelly but still soft to eat. It dissolved as much as was chewed. I liked it a lot.

"I don't know what this is, but I like it," he said. His mouth was full and his hand was dripping the jelly onto the floor between us. I put my hand in and grabbed some more. It wasn't long before the contents of the jar had been transported to our stomachs. We both had smiles on our faces.

"What are we going to do with the jar?" I asked. I hadn't thought this far in advance.

"We can take it outside and throw it somewhere where they won't find it." Geezis always had an answer. So that's what we did.

We left the other jar full of pickles unopened under my pillow. We put on our outside clothes and went outside. It was cold, the type where your eyelashes froze. I noticed his hair that crossed his face was white with little frozen ice crystals. I wish I had hair that was long like that. We made our way to the edge of the school yard, near some bushes, and threw the glass jar as far as we could. We were laughing and enjoying ourselves but it was too cold to do more than what we set out to. We quickly returned to the dorm.

As we opened the heavy front doors, we saw the figure of Brother Nicholas.

"Having fun this Christmas?" he said.

"Yes, Brother Nicholas." We both said it at the same time.

"Find any fun games to play?"

Geezis couldn't look him in the eye and had become very quiet. I was feeling guilty about our theft and wasn't sure what to say. I decided to say nothing.

Brother Nicholas's face lost its caring look. He grabbed our shoulders and moved his face closer. "I smelled something when I walked past your room. I figured it must be something serious if I could smell it in a room with over fifty beds, so I walked in. Do you know what I found?"

The two of us shook our heads.

"I followed my nose to some mess on the floor. It smelled like fish. I couldn't understand how that could be. I searched the beds and found a jar of pickles under a pillow. I know I didn't authorize that. I don't know how it could have magically made its way from the kitchen to a boy's pillow." He stopped to look at us closely.

"You wouldn't happen to know whose beds those could be?"

I looked involuntarily at Geezis but his eyes were on the floor. He had gone quiet. I was relying on him to get us out of this situation. I felt my shoulder being squeezed harder by the brother.

"It was me. It's my bed."

"Very good, David. But I'm sure that you weren't alone in your thieving, were you?"

I was quiet. I didn't look at him.

"Let me guess. Was Joseph your accomplice?" He squeezed us until we both began to wilt at the knees.

"Yes." It was quiet, but it came from Geezis.

"Good. David, you run along. I will have a word with our friend Joseph alone."

I looked quickly at Geezis and then ran up the stairs. When I turned to look back, the brother had his arm around Geezis and was leading him downstairs.

It was dark when he returned. All the boys were in bed and I was waiting for him. He walked as though he was in a lot of pain but didn't say a word. He got under his covers and turned away from me. At least Brother Nicholas left the jar of pickles for us.

*

More children arrived at the school after Christmas. The beds were all full again. Some boys coughed. I began to notice the coughs. Many of the girls also coughed. I didn't see the older boys or girls, so I don't know about them. By March, the room with sick kids was full again.

"I wonder if they'll go to the same place as the other kids," I said. Geezis was on the swing next to me chewing on a piece of tree that he broke off from a branch.

"Dunno. I guess we'll be seeing more burials."

"You think the others died?"

"What else could have happened?"

I didn't know how he knew so much. "Maybe they were sent home."

"They were coughing blood. I saw it myself." He said it matter-of-factly.

"When did you see them last?"

"Brother Nicholas would take me there on occasion. He would make me kneel and pray with him. They are being consumed, he told me."

"Consumed by who?"

"I dunno. Maybe Jesus? Maybe that's how God gets them back."

That made me think. He always came up with the deep ideas.

He was right about one thing. The burials began happening more often. More burials, more sick kids. No doctors.

By May, the routine had become second nature to me. Every morning began with washing up and prayers, then cold porridge mush, then classes, then a soupy lunch, then working outside. Dinner was the same boiled meat and potato; sometimes rancid, mainly OK. It felt like we prayed non-stop. Before eating, after eating. Before bed, and when we woke up. On Sunday, it was worse. Two hours of prayer and church service. We had to confess our sins and then go back to do it all over again the following week. I was beginning to ache to go home. I needed to see my parents. It was nine months since I saw them last. Three full seasons had passed—autumn, winter and spring. One more month of school before summer holidays.

Geezis and I did everything together. I didn't have an older brother. I had two sisters and a young brother. I was three years older than the oldest. I thought of my sisters when I saw the older girls cleaning the outside windows.

"Do you think they're playing or is that work?"

Geezis looked up at the top floor of the dorm. The window was open and a girl was on the ledge, cleaning the window. We both had to look carefully to see the rope that was tied around her waist. We couldn't see who was holding on to it from the inside. "If it's playing, it looks scary."

We were pulling the weeds from the garden. We had planted it earlier in the month and the weeds were the only thing that I could see growing. The older boys were in the fields. They got to work with the horses. They tried to deal with one acre per day. That meant when it came time to harvesting, they would have to stagger the collections and hope the weather cooperated. It looked like hard work. I was happy with pulling weeds.

I saw Geezis looking at the girl washing the window. I also found myself looking at her. While we pulled weeds, she managed to do the entire top floor. We saw her disappear and then pop out at the next window. We always knew which one because it had to open first.

Later that evening, Geezis disappeared from his bed. I was used to this by now. In the past, I asked him where he went. He would just shrug and say that he was walking around. It happened a few times every week. But he always came back. He didn't notice, but I would stay awake until he returned. That's how I knew. I couldn't sleep until I knew he was back. Once in a while, I fell asleep waiting. Not tonight.

The sun had just set and it was late. There was a full moon out. It gave a silver glow to the room. I liked the way I could recognize everyone but they all looked different. I got up and decided to find him. The rest of the boys were either sleeping or supposed to be sleeping. I knew I needed to avoid being caught. I hadn't been given the strap for a couple of weeks and I didn't feel like going to bed with that type of burning pain.

I went to the kitchen first. I assumed he would have been looking for a snack. Then, I popped my head into the laundry room and play rooms. Nothing. I went to our floor and checked out the sick kids' room. Nothing there. I crept up to the floor above us, where the older kids slept. Nothing. The brothers and nuns slept on the floor above but there was no way he'd be up there. But, as he wasn't below, I decided to keep going up. I knew I had to be extra quiet.

I had never been to the top of the building before. It looked like our floor, but there were more doors. Perhaps they didn't all sleep in the same room. I became like a shadow. I didn't want to make a sound. I kept looking for places to hide if a door opened. There weren't any. I walked down the hallway, taking in all the different smells from the floor. There was the smell of tobacco; I know Father O'Flaherty smoked. Maybe others did as well. I saw some flowers and thought that was where the sisters must be sleeping. There were windows at the end of each hall and the moonlight made things just visible enough. My main concern was not bumping into anything or knocking something over.

I was half way down the hallway when I saw a small silhouette set out against the moonlight. I assumed it was Geezis and started going faster. He didn't see me approaching. He was looking out the window at something. Then he opened it and stepped onto the ledge. I began to run.

"Geezis," I whispered as loudly as I could without speaking.

He turned around and saw me. I was now less than five feet away.

"Hi, Migizi." He didn't say anything else. His face showed no emotion. He turned away from me and jumped.

⁂

I don't remember what I did after that. I must have screamed because doors began to open and angry nuns and brothers began to appear. When Father O'Flaherty arrived, I was crying and he picked me up and carried me to his room. He told me to go to sleep and he would see what happened. He didn't want me to go back and disturb the other boys.

All I could see was the dull colour of Geezis' hair in the moonlight as he disappeared from sight. What would cause him to do that? He was my best friend, my only friend. I didn't understand.

It was also the first day that I heard the drums.

CHAPTER FIVE

Of Indians and Dogs

"David!"

"Yes, sir," I said.

"Do you think you can pick those rows first?"

"Yes, sir."

"I'll have the rest of the crew move over there to help you when they're finished. Kim found some good ones in there, didn't you sweetheart?"

"Yes, Daddy." She hid behind her father as he spoke to me. She was a little younger than me, probably around sixteen. I had never seen a girl look like that before. She had white-blonde hair and was almost as tall as me.

I got my pails off the back of the wagon and went where Mr. Thiessen pointed. It was easy work and I was able to eat enough so that I never felt hungry. But strawberry picking was a new crop for him and I was glad to get the job after school finished. The rest of his farm was a combination of the usual potatoes and beets. Wheat was grown on the land that couldn't grow the former. It was 1926, a good year for Canada, but we still suffered where I lived. Every dollar helped.

There was a balance between speed and damaging the berries. You had to have soft hands, as Mr. Thiessen said, and those who didn't were fired pretty quickly. I put the pail on the ground and bent down on one knee and began. I would make my way down the row on my one knee, using my planted foot to sort of walk. It must have looked funny, but it worked for me.

"Do you need a hand?"

I looked up to see Kimberley. "No, thanks. I'm OK."

"I can take your full buckets back to the wagon and bring you fresh ones. It's no trouble at all."

I didn't want to contradict the boss's daughter so I nodded. I returned to my picking and the full pails were whisked away and empty ones brought back. It meant I didn't get a break in my picking. I liked the walk back to the wagon. It made my back less sore.

"You've been working long like this?"

"No. Just finished school."

"Me, too. I'm not sure what I'm supposed to do now."

"What do you mean? You're rich. You don't need to do anything."

She laughed, and it was the nicest sound I had ever heard. I tried to keep picking while she talked or else I wouldn't fill my quota. Mr. Thiessen didn't care what you looked like or where you were from but he did care about his crops being harvested.

"We're farmers. We're not rich."

"You have land and you grow things. And you sell those things for money."

"I don't know about all that." She smiled and I could see she didn't have a care in the world. It made me feel good inside, despite my own situation.

"Are you here for the rest of the summer?" I don't know why I asked the question. I wasn't sure why she was even talking to me.

Her white face became slightly red in the neck and cheeks. "Yes." She squirmed and began to fidget. "You?"

I laughed. "I'm not going anywhere, Miss Thiessen."

"Kim, please. And you are?"

"David." I used the name the school gave me.

"Nice to meet you, David. Some friends and I are going to a church function on Saturday. Do you want to come?"

I felt a liquid movement in my chest and gut. I wanted to go but I knew I wouldn't belong. "Thanks. But, I don't think I can make it."

Her eyes moved to the ground and traced the area where I was working. "When do you think you can make it?"

"I dunno. What do you do at these church events?"

"Sing. Play games. There are about twenty of us. My father is also the pastor at the church. I'm sure he won't have a problem with you joining us."

I hesitated. It didn't feel right. "I'm not sure, Kim. I don't want to get in trouble with your dad."

"I'll tell you what. I'll ask him and, if he says it's OK, will you come?"

I didn't have a choice. "Of course."

She ran off towards her dad. I could swear she ran on her tiptoes. I continued picking but I developed a burning sensation on my back as I could sense them looking at me. I turned my body so I could see their conversation. Kim was animated, arms moving all over the place. Mr. Thiessen stood stationary with his head bent to get closer to her. I could see his head shaking 'no'. Then more arm movements from Kim and a couple of stomps with her foot. I saw Mr. Thiessen close his eyes and shrug. I could imagine the 'OK' from where I was picking. I turned fully back to my picking when I realized they had stopped talking.

"You can come this Saturday after work. The rest of us are getting together at the church at noon, but I know you need to work. We'll still be there until at least eight or nine." She had started talking as though there was no break in time from when she left to when she returned. She didn't even bother that I had my back turned towards her.

"I'll be dirty from work. I can't show up like this," I said. I looked at my hands compared to hers. Mine were already looking dry and worn. Hers looked unused.

"You'll be fine. You can shower and change at the church. There's plenty of clothes donated that sits in boxes. You can take some and see what fits."

It didn't feel right. I knew I should say no. But I couldn't say no to the boss's daughter. "I'll be there," I said.

She smiled, and all my concerns melted away.

It was another three days before Saturday arrived. I brought a change of clothes in a bag as I didn't want her to think I was a charity case. Work was hard and my back ached. We started at six in the morning and finished at four in the afternoon. I caught a ride into town with one of the older workers who shook his head when I told him where I was going. I ignored him.

"You made it!" Kim burst into a smile as soon as she saw me walk around the corner looking for her. The rest of her friends were playing some ball game with pieces of bright cloth on the side of their trousers. She looked like she wanted to hug me but I moved away. "Follow me," she said.

I followed her around to the side of the church and into an area where they had a changing room, showers, and toilets.

"This is pretty good for a church," I said.

"We do everything here. You know how the winter is. We end up playing indoors when the cold becomes too much."

"Nice."

"Oh, I guess I'll leave you to change. Do you need any clothes?"

"I brought my own."

"OK. See you outside."

I watched her leave and could feel myself wanting her to stay. I showered and changed as quickly as I could. Holding my dirty clothes, I retraced my steps to where they were playing and put my things in a pile out of the way. Kim saw me and waved me to come over to her.

"Everyone, this is David. He is my new friend. He works with me and my dad. David, this is everyone."

I nodded and shook the odd hand. They seemed to be happy that I came. I didn't know what I was worried about. I listened to the rules of the game and joined Kim's side. She kept looking back at me and smiling. I smiled back.

I came back the next day for Sunday school and the church service where everyone attended. It wasn't like mass at school. It was spoken in English and there was no eating of the body of Christ nor drinking of his blood.

I didn't notice any of this at first because Kim sat next to me. Every once in a while, her leg would touch mine and I couldn't concentrate on her father talking at the front. I stood and sang when everyone else did. I enjoyed sharing the hymn book with Kim more than singing. It meant that even her arms touched me. Sometimes, I felt her finger brush against mine. I could smell her clean hair and it made me conscious of how I must have looked. The next Sunday, I made sure I had scrubbed cleaner than I had ever done before.

"How's your girlfriend?" Binesi asked. His school name was Thomas, and he was nineteen and already had a child of his own.

"She's not my girlfriend," I said. I felt the heat on my neck as I said it.

"She sees you almost every day."

"Yes," I said.

"She comes all the way to the fields and waits for you to finish work so that you can walk her home.

"Yes."

"You play with her friends and sit next to her at church?"

"Yes."

"Then, she's your girlfriend." The other workers laughed along with Thomas. I didn't say anything. Strawberry season was done and we were trying to finish this field of baby potatoes. By September, the sugar beets would be coming into season. Talking slowed us down.

"What do you think will happen?" Thomas continued.

I didn't say anything. I kept my head down and shoved the potato shovel into the earth. It was like a normal shovel but it had gaps in it to allow the earth to shake out and made collecting potatoes a lot easier. It was like a fork but with no pointy bits that might bruise the potatoes.

"Have you kissed her yet?"

"Shut up, Thomas."

"I'll take that as a no."

"It's not like that."

"Have you held hands?"

I was silent.

"Do you think you'll get married? Have nice little white kids? Live happily ever after?"

I didn't want to respond. I wanted to hit him and make him shut up. But I didn't want to lose my job and not see Kim again.

"What does Mr. Thiessen think of your love affair? Is he happy?"

"I'm still working here," I said finally. "And he's a pastor. He's not like the priests and nuns; he sees me as a person."

"Keep telling yourself that, David." He was faster than me with the potatoes and was able to talk and keep ahead of me so it didn't look like he was being lazy. It made me even angrier.

I blocked him out and focused on finishing my row, and then the field. I needed the money.

Four o'clock came and Kim was waiting for me. She wore a light summer dress even though it was closer to autumn and she smiled whenever she looked at me. I shook off as much of the dust and mud as I could and we started walking. It was the best part of the day for me. The sun was shining bright, there were no clouds, and she would talk about things she had done that day and what she wanted to do in the future.

"And Hannah got engaged to John yesterday. That was something we all knew was going to happen, but she still acted surprised." Kim was animated as she spoke. I could see her red lips against her white teeth. Every once in a while, I could see her tongue peek out from behind her teeth as her smile would interrupt her talking.

"When are you going to university?" I asked. It weighed heavily on me.

"Next week. I don't know what changed my daddy's mind. He always said I should get married and settle down. It's not really a university, you know. More of a theology college."

"Is it far?"

"A day's drive. Maybe longer."

"Will you be coming home often?"

"As often as I can."

I felt a falling feeling inside as though I was looking at the end of our friendship. She was holding my hand and I could see the mud that had rubbed off onto hers.

"Why'd you stop?" she asked.

"To do this." I leaned in and kissed her. I had never kissed anyone before, so I don't know if I did it right. I just made sure my lips touched hers. Then, I backed away to see what she would do.

Her eyes were closed for a while and her face reddened. "I was wondering when you would do that," she said.

It was the last thing I expected. Then she kissed me back, this time longer. I didn't want to touch her dress with my dirty hands, so I stood there with one hand in hers and the other by my side. I could feel my body begin to shake and I got very hot. I could see that she was also very red. We turned and continued walking. I replayed that kiss over and over in my head and wondered when I could do it again.

We reached the town and she let go of my hand. We weren't officially boyfriend and girlfriend so we didn't hold hands in town. I saw her to her door and waved goodbye. There definitely wouldn't be any kissing where people could see us. I then began the two-hour walk back home. This time, I didn't remember anything after the wave to when I arrived home. All I could think about was that kiss.

*
*

The next day, Kim didn't arrive at four and I went home instead. She didn't show up the day after, either. I heard from Mr. Thiessen that she had already left for university. When I heard the news, I felt as though someone had opened up a tap on my leg and all my energy drained out.

Winter arrived and Mr. Thiessen didn't need us for anything and I had no other work. I did odd jobs with my uncle and Thomas, but nothing steady.

"Where do you think you're going?" Thomas said. I was wearing my Sunday best and walking towards town.

"It's Thanksgiving. She'll be back to visit. I'm going to see Kim."

Thomas wasn't mocking. His face looked concerned. "Don't go, David. Let her go."

"She loves me and I love her." I felt foolish saying the words, but I meant them.

"She may love you but her father doesn't. You won't be allowed to love her, my friend."

I could see Thomas was being serious and I felt a degree of dread inside of me. "If that's how it's going to be, I want to hear it directly from her." I continued in the direction I was going and soon I was alone on the dirt road that led from the reserve to the town.

When I finally arrived, I was sweating despite the cold. The door hurt my hand as I knocked. I waited, a step back in order to allow the screen door to open. It wasn't long before Mr. Thiessen's body filled the door.

"David."

"Sir."

"How can I help you?"

"I was wondering whether Kim came back for the holidays."

I saw something cross his face, then, "No."

I felt his answer like the branches that slapped my face when I was young and followed my father in the bush. I stood there, saying nothing. Neither did Mr. Thiessen.

I don't know how long we stood in silence before I noticed Mr. Thiessen begin to back away, causing the screen door to close. As he turned and closed the heavy internal wood door, I thought I saw a glimpse of a dress Kim would have worn. I stood like a lump on the doorsteps. It began to rain and I decided to return home.

I knew I would see her at Christmas. I hadn't received a postcard or letter from her, but I didn't think much of it. I didn't send her one either.

⁑

Christmas was very much like Thanksgiving, except I knew she was there. I stood on the steps and asked my question. Mr. Thiessen provided his response. We looked at each other and then he went back inside and I left. This time, I decided I would wait and see what Kim had to say for herself. I dressed with the warmest furs my father would let me have and I waited.

I saw the movements of the family inside, the candles lit as the sun went down, and the candles extinguished when the family went to bed. I knew which room was Kim's and I found some pebbles to throw at her window. My heart jumped into my throat when I saw the window slide open.

"Hello?" She stuck her head out the window and whispered loudly.

"Kim," I whispered back. "It's me. David." I moved out of the shadows into the silver of the half-moon light.

She smiled and I knew everything would be OK. "Why didn't you come earlier?"

"I did. Your father said you weren't here."

Her face clouded but then cleared. "You're here now and that's what matters." I wasn't sure if she misheard me but I was pleased to see her. All I could think about was kissing her.

"Can you come down?"

"Now? Never. I'll be cloistered until I'm twenty-five!" She laughed softly.

"Can I see you tomorrow?"

"Yes!"

"What time?"

"Come for lunch. I'll make sure I answer any knocks on the door."

"I'll see you there." I wanted to whoop but I closed my jacket closer to me and waved good night. I saw the window close and all was still again.

The next day, Kim answered the door and I could smell the cooked meat and vegetables fresh from the oven. My mouth began to water. My hands also began sweating as she took me by the hand into the parlour where her parents were sitting. I saw Mr. and Mrs. Thiessen's faces but it is hard to describe the emotions or expressions as they seemed to display them all. I regretted my sweaty palm when I walked over and shook their hands. Each one of them had to wipe their hand on their clothes afterwards.

The meal was quiet. All I can remember was the sound of the cutlery against the plates. Mr. Thiessen didn't say a word other than the prayer at the beginning. Mrs. Thiessen busied herself with the food without saying a word to me. I didn't care as Kim sat beaming next to me, oblivious to her parents and family. All her brothers ate in silence, too.

I was pleased to leave the house with Kim and two of her brothers. We decided to walk off the meal. I was hoping to be alone with Kim but her parents demanded that she be chaperoned. I knew what it meant—I wasn't able to hold her hand or kiss her.

My visit finished too quickly as did the holidays. I saw Kim every day. We even snuck out one day, hand in hand, and walked for hours. I think she got in trouble for that and she left for school the next day. I would have to wait until she returned.

*
*

Spring arrived and I couldn't wait to see Kim. My head was full of images of her and me together, getting married and living on the farm. I was a good worker. It made sense for her to marry me. We could have a good family. I decided to ask her father's permission before I asked her. It was the right thing to do.

"You want to *what?*" Mr. Thiessen was a gentle man who knew how to work. As a boss, he was hard but fair. As a pastor, he had a full church. As a father, he had a happy family. I looked forward to joining his family.

"I would like your blessing to ask your daughter to marry me," I said.

He grew silent and I could hear the ragged breath through his nose. "You're a good boy, David, and a hard worker. I appreciate that about you."

I sat taller with the compliment.

"I've noticed you spending a lot of time with my daughter."

"She is incredible, sir."

"Yes, I know. I taught her to see the man and not their skin."

I began to have a bad feeling about this. I said nothing.

"She's young. She doesn't understand."

"Sir?"

"She doesn't know how the world works. I won't be here forever and I need someone to protect her. She's innocent."

I don't know why he was telling me this. I knew that the world was tough. I have eyes and can see what goes on in the reserve and what went on in the school. There are bad people in the world. No news there.

He put his hand on my shoulder and left it there. "David, I can't give you my blessing. I'm sorry. I hope you understand."

"Sir?"

"You know how things are. I want my daughter to have children and to be part of the community."

"We can have children."

"I'm sorry, David. I know you're sweet on her and maybe she's sweet on you. But this is my decision."

I couldn't speak. His hand was still on me. His voice was friendly but matter-of-fact. I didn't even think that this was possible. I blinked my eyes as he became blurry. I nodded and thanked him for his time, and left.

I couldn't breathe properly as my chest began to close. My legs tingled and went numb. I don't know how I managed to walk home. I lay down and didn't move for hours. My parents didn't disturb me until the following day when they shooed me outside. They said it wasn't healthy for me to mope around. I knew Kim was arriving today so I decided to see what she thought about this.

There was an awkward moment when Mr. Thiessen opened the door. I saw his eyes widen and then narrow. He called Kim and let us talk on the porch.

"You look pretty today," I said. She did.

"Thanks."

"How are your studies going?"

"OK."

"Are you here for the summer or...?"

"I'm here until the fall."

I never had this much trouble speaking to her in the past. She wasn't smiling either. I kept silent for a moment, hoping she would open up.

"My daddy talked to me."

I felt a burning in my chest. I waited.

"He said you asked him for my hand." Her eyes had welled up and a single tear crossed her cheek. She wiped it away with the back of her hand.

"I ... I love you, Kim."

She lowered her head. "I know. I think I love you, too." Her tears were now two lines that ran from her eyes down to her chin

I held my breath. I inched my hand closer to hers, enough for our fingers to touch. I couldn't hold her hand in front of her house.

"I can't see you any more, David." She said the words and walked away.

I heard the door open and close. I couldn't move initially and I don't know how long I stood there. Eventually, I could feel the spring air against my skin and I knew it was time to leave her alone.

Mr. Thiessen kept me on and I worked doubly hard. There were a lot of us at times but only a handful stayed on from the turning of the soil and planting all the way to the harvesting and burning off the stubble. I felt privileged to be part of the core group. I was determined to show Mr. Thiessen that I was worthy of his daughter's hand.

Kim didn't come every day at four like she used to, but I saw her from time to time. She even let me walk her home a couple of times. By late July, she let me hold her hand again. She led me into the field of maize and kissed me. I thought my body was going to explode with the energy she gave me. I knew I had a chance as long as she loved me. Her father would learn to like me as well.

Harvest time was a big deal this year. The weather was good and the crops filled every truck and basket we could find. Mr. Thiessen abandoned the strawberries and focused on his other crops. He even had a tractor that he rode in the town's annual festival parade. The tractor made everything easier. I was hoping to be able to use it next year.

Kim was coming every day to meet me again and her father noticed. He didn't say anything. He must have seen us holding hands.

"Yes."

"Sorry?"

"Yes, I'll marry you." She had her beaming smile on and her eyes danced with the light.

"But your father—"

"He'll come around. You'll see."

She was leaving for school tomorrow and we were walking slowly down one of the dirt roads near town. I hadn't asked her to marry me and never raised the subject after her father made his position so clear.

"I hope so. I'm doing my best." I couldn't say anything else as she was already kissing me. I felt nervous about being seen but that thought left me as her hands touched my face. I felt her whole body push up against me and all I wanted was her.

It was a long while before we reached her house. It was odd to wave to her as she disappeared inside, especially as we were kissing earlier. I walked on clouds as the town passed my sight and the fields opened up in front of me. I was roughly half way home when I heard the sound of Mr. Thiessen's Model T coming from behind me. It must be a special occasion for him to be driving it. He bought it after the harvest for two hundred and sixty dollars. There were quite a few cars in town already but he was the only person I knew who owned one. I turned around and waved to him.

The car stopped next to me and I saw Mr. Thiessen driving plus three large men I didn't know. They all got out of the car and approached me.

"'Afternoon, Mr. Thiessen."

"Hello, David."

"That's a fine vehicle you have, sir."

He didn't reply immediately. "David, I thought we had an understanding."

"About what?"

"My daughter." He was looking directly at me as were the three men behind him.

I got a bad feeling all of a sudden.

"Kim?"

"You know what I'm talking about."

"I haven't done anything wrong, sir. Honest."

"David, do you have a dog?"

"No, sir."

"Well, let me tell you something about dogs. They need to be trained. Even the best dogs are still dogs. They need to be disciplined. You can talk to them and be kind to them but, sometimes, you need to show them who's boss."

I saw the three men holding something in their hands. I couldn't make it out. I was planted to the earth. I felt the wind speak something to me but I couldn't catch it.

"Sir?"

"I told you to stay away from my daughter." He nodded to the boys who showed me what they held in their hands. Each one held a strap.

I felt the hand of one of them grab me before I had the sense to run. The other two began hitting me with the strap. On the legs, then my back and arms. It hurt but I had received worse at school—or, at least, I felt I had received worse. This pain was different. I felt betrayed. It took a moment before I realized Mr. Thiessen was talking to me. I was lying on the road. I knew I would be badly bruised from this beating but the hardest hits came from his mouth.

"I love all of God's creations, but Indians and whites don't mix. I have asked you kindly. I have now educated you on your skin. Don't make me talk to you again. Don't forget who you are, David. You're an Indian. Find an Indian girl. Leave my daughter alone."

I heard the gurgling sound of the car as it turned around and then disappeared into the distance. I was in too much pain to cry. I stood up, pointed myself in the direction of home, and walked. The tears came. I knew the pain would go away. I wasn't sure about the hurt.

CHAPTER SIX

Dampening the Pain and Memories

"I don't care about that. Get out there and find a job." Theresa kicked my feet off the stool and glowered above me.

"I can't help it if there aren't any jobs," I said.

"You seemed to be doing well enough when I first met you. What happened?"

"I don't know. No one has jobs anymore."

"David, I love you. You are the father of our children. But you need to find a way to feed them."

I got up, still feeling the effects of the night before. I couldn't handle the nagging. It never stopped. Then, as if on cue, the baby started crying. That set off the other. I had enough and left without a word.

It was five years since I was reminded of who I was. What I was. An Indian. No better than a dog. Kim stopped seeing me and I wasn't keen on getting another beating like that anytime soon. I went to a party with my uncles and met Theresa. She is an Indian. Like me. Only pregnant all the time.

I arrived at my uncle's house and went inside. It was only four doors away. Everyone was still sleeping. I found some remaining beer and opened one up. It felt good. After the second, my headache and aches disappeared. They would be up soon enough and I could see there was still enough to drink for all of us. I decided to stay. It was peaceful compared to home.

They say that Prime Minister Bennett was doing the best he could. To tell you the truth, I couldn't tell the difference. Nothing changed for me. I was an Indian. I was supposed to stay on the reserve. If I wanted to leave, I had to get a pass. I got arrested once because of it; I thought it was because of Mr. Thiessen. No one told me about the pass—until the RCMP pulled me over.

That was 1930. It was a tough year for me and this year looked to be even tougher. Theresa used to be fun but has become miserable whenever I am around. She even refuses to lie with me until I get a job. And number three is due any moment now.

I miss Kim. I miss working in Mr. Thiessen's fields. I miss earning my own money. I don't like my life. We live in shacks compared to the home of Mr. Thiessen. Each summer, we mix the earth and fill the cracks in the walls of our house. We still have a house made of logs and it needs constant attention if we hope to keep the winter wind out. I didn't mind until I met Kim. Until then, it was all I knew. Kim showed me what I was missing. I realized I wasn't a man. Mr. Thiessen was right.

Thomas and I became friends. I was now twenty-one and had learned a thing or two about life. He helped me when I was the angriest. He took me to parties, introduced me to Theresa and let me smoke his pipe. It made me feel better, dampening the pain and memories. I found some more of his herbs and lit up now as I waited for them to wake up. I didn't understand how they could sleep so long.

"Is that you, David?" It was a familiar voice.

I turned around. "Yeah."

"Give me what you're having, eh?"

"Both?"

She smiled. "I'll take the smoke to start. I'll take your beer. You can get yourself some more." She was stretching and I could see her curves beneath the layers she wore. My mind took a while to snap back to the present.

"Uh, OK. Here."

She took a deep drag on the smoke and closed her eyes. She held it in her lungs and then released the smoke through her nose and mouth. She drank while smoke was still coming out of her. I thought it looked pretty amazing.

"Looks like I missed a party," I said. I had found another beer and smoke. Thomas was good that way. His herbs were already rolled and his beer was cold.

"Howard was arrested," she said instead.

"Why?"

"Got caught with alcohol."

"Did they keep him?"

"Yeah."

"So Thomas decided to throw a party?"

She grinned as the smoke passed her lips and hiccupped. "Where'd he get so much stuff?"

"He just does." She came closer to me. I was already sitting on the floor and she sat next to me.

"Any news on work?" I needed money and living on the Res wasn't going to get me anything more than charity from the government.

She laughed again. "None." She had finished my first beer and took my second from me. She kissed me in exchange.

"I'll get another."

"Stay," she held me close to her.

I did.

*

When I returned home, Theresa was stomping around in a foul mood.

"You have fun?" she said. It was what she didn't say that spoke volumes.

"Yeah."

"Find a job?"

"How could I find a job at Thomas's?"

"Exactly. You go and drink your life away while your babies are starving. Don't you have any decency?"

I was feeling guilty about more than a few drinks so I kept quiet. She spoke for both of us.

"Don't you want to be a father? Or are you some no good drunk Indian, just like the others? Is that what I've done? I've found myself a drunk and a good for nothing Indian." She said *'Indian'* like she was spitting.

I shrugged my shoulders. I was feeling pretty good until I came home.

"Maybe you should find yourself another home, another squaw to lie with and to lie to. You're nothing but a worthless—"

She didn't finish because she was on the ground. I don't know how I did it but my hand was raised, looking to hit her again. She looked back at me with rage in her eyes. It wasn't the first time I had hit her and I had sworn I would never do it again.

"Oh, big Indian man. Hit your wife. Why don't you hit your kids as well? They haven't had a beating for a while. What reason today? You don't like the colour of the sun? Or maybe I'm not walking sexy-like enough for you? Or maybe you haven't had enough fire water in your body? Or too much? Huh? What is it this time?"

I hit her again. I took off my belt and began to beat her with it. The babies were screaming, Theresa was screaming, and I was screaming. I knew how to do it; the sisters and brothers did it often enough to us. They helped me become the man I was.

I hit her again, this time on the leg. Then on the thigh. She turned her back and I hit her as hard as I could along the back with the strap. I stopped when she stopped screaming and lay curled up like a child, whimpering.

"I don't want to hear you say those things to me ever again," I said.

She didn't reply. She was rocking silently to herself.

I looked at our home and suddenly felt like a stranger. The walls were something out of a settler's first cabin, not someone living in the 1930s. We had nothing compared to Kim's home. I looked at my wife and saw the raw hands made red from hard work. I saw baby Makwa in his crib and heard his cry. I didn't know where Asin was but I knew he was somewhere. Maybe hiding behind the door to my bedroom.

I gathered my boots, my jacket, and the money I kept for emergencies. I slammed the door behind me and began walking. I walked away from my home, out of the reserve, and towards the railway line. I needed freedom and it wasn't to be found on the Res.

It was a good time of year to walk. The snow had melted long ago and the ground was firm. It took me three days to get to the railway. I walked the first day on anger alone. I don't know how far I walked but I stopped when I was sore. I slept beneath the stars. I never worried about any animal hurting me. I was always lucky that way.

By the second day, my thirst was becoming an issue. I came across a farm and they gave me some water and food. The man of the house wasn't in so the wife put the food and water outside the other entrance to the home and told me to wait where I was. She spoke to me through the window screen.

When she felt safe and locked up nicely in the house, she said I could go around and get it. I did and I thanked her for it. There was enough for me to take extra bread and meat for the following day.

When I reached the railway line, I didn't know what I wanted to do. The whole thing seemed stupid by now and I began to think I should return to the Res. Then I saw an image of Theresa's face as she looked at me and decided it would be better if I never returned. I began walking south, towards Winnipeg.

It was longer than I anticipated and I soon became worried about my lack of water as I hadn't had a drink for more than a day by now. I saw some houses in the distance and said a quick prayer of thanks to Jesus for helping me in my time of need. In the distance, I could see a raven floating, then flying, in the air. It soared and I began to think it was an eagle, then it disappeared from my sight.

"Hello friends," I said. The men stopped working as I approached and held their tools by their sides. "I'm looking for work and was hoping you may have something?"

The four workers turned towards a man I couldn't see properly. I assumed he must have been their boss. He walked forward and looked carefully at me.

"Where you from?" he asked.

"Seven days' walk from here," I said. "I'm heading to Winnipeg to look for work. I need some food and water and I've never begged for anything in my life. I need some work now to get me those things."

The boss nodded appreciatively. "I like that. I could use a man like you for a few days if that helps. I'll feed you first. Can't work on an empty stomach. Can you frame?"

I didn't know what that was. "No, sir."

"Have you done any construction?"

"No, sir. But I do know agriculture."

He laughed. "I don't have a farm, son. I need to build these two homes before the snow flies. You look strong and I could use a hand. I can't pay you much but it'll be enough for food and shelter and will leave you with a few bucks in your pocket when you leave. How's that?"

"That sounds good to me, sir." I put my hand out and he shook it. He had rough hands and strong, like a vice.

"OK, boys, back to work. Son, what's your name?"

"David, sir."

"Good to meet you, David. I'm Bjorn. Follow me to the house and we'll get you set up. Freja will get some hot food into you and some soup and you'll be right as rain. Sleeping is in the barn, if that's OK with you. I've got a family, so I don't let anyone in the house." He was talking and was relaxed but his eyes watched me carefully.

"I'd like that, sir. I've been sleeping under the stars so a barn is luxury."

"I'm going to like you, David," he said. He patted me on the back as we made our way to his home.

*
*

I stayed for two months at Bjorn's place. It was hard work but I got fed and slept in the barn with the other guys. They weren't as friendly as Bjorn. Two were from Mexico and barely spoke English. The other two rarely spoke and seemed hostile towards me. None of us were from that town.

The creosoted wood with metal rails stretched in front of me as far as I could see. I was at least ten days' walk from Winnipeg and I had enough money to live on until I got there. I hoped to find a job and make some money; maybe even send for Theresa.

The bottoms of my feet began to ache as I walked from railroad tie to tie. I tried walking on the granite stones instead and that hurt my feet even more.

Walking on the rail itself was the least painful for the feet but it was hard not to fall off. I occupied myself with these concerns as it passed the time.

I purchased a water bottle and was able to conserve water to last me three, sometimes four days. I always came across a town before then.

The autumn was creeping in and I could see the harvested fields. I stayed at Bjorn's too long and had missed the harvesting jobs. I didn't mind. I knew I would find something in Winnipeg that would solve my problems.

Not knowing where to go, I went to the city centre.

"Sorry. Unions only."

"No work here today. Try next week."

"You have a trade? No? Sorry, we've got enough labourers."

I stopped at every construction site, blacksmith and building that looked like it may have work. I wasn't worried. I hadn't been trying long. I was confident that I would find a job. After sleeping on the banks of the Red River for two nights, I became a little more desperate.

"Sir, I'll work for food." I had found the boss of a construction site and he was willing to see me. I didn't want to blow it, so I asked for the bare minimum. I needed to stay alive. To do that, I needed food.

"What can you do?" His English was barely better than mine. He was a big man, a good four inches taller than me and he looked like he could wrestle a bear.

"I know farming," I said. "They taught me that in school. I did some work on a construction site building two houses. I mainly did what I was told to do."

"I can't be hand holding," he said. He was measuring me, trying to determine whether I could handle the work.

"I will do what you ask me to, sir," I said.

"OK," he said slowly. He rubbed his chin and his forearm muscles rippled. His shirt was rolled up past the elbow. "I'll give you a shovel. It's hard work. If you last a week, we'll talk."

"Thank you, sir. You won't regret it." I held my hand out to shake his. It was met with a vice-like grip that made me think he should have been working with steel instead of wood.

"See you tomorrow. If you're late, don't bother coming." He nodded and turned to a guy with white dust all over him and began discussing something I couldn't hear.

I felt a jolt of warmth as the good news sunk in. I didn't have a place to sleep but I had a job. We didn't talk money; I assumed he would pay me in food or come to some arrangement after a week. I didn't care. I was over the moon.

That night, I made my way to the water's edge to set up camp. It wasn't far from the work site and I always felt better under the trees and sky than in some corner of a building or street. I scanned the bushes for berries and realized the birds hadn't cleaned them out. I began picking and eating until my face was stained with blueberries and blackberries. I picked until my travelling satchel was full. I then picked until I had enough for a present to my new boss the next day.

"Boss, I just wanted to say thank you again for giving me a job," I said. "Here. I picked them for you."

He looked at the piece of fabric with the berries inside. At first, I thought he was disgusted at my gift or the fabric. I couldn't read him. "Thank you. What's your name again?"

"David."

"Thank you, David. My wife loves berries and will make this into something wonderful. By the way, don't call me boss. Call me Mike." He caressed the berries as I handed them to him, careful not to bruise or crush them. He then took them and put them into his lunch box. "Safest place," he said when he realized I was watching him.

"OK, boss, I mean, Mike." I felt good and returned to my shovelling. I was part of a ten-man crew digging a basement. At least it looked like a basement. To me, it was a hole in the ground.

The next day, I was called over.

"Yes, Mike?" I said.

"Here. My wife made the most amazing pie and I thought you should have some of it." He gave me money at the end of yesterday's work day so I wasn't sure if this pie was payment for today's work. He must have seen the look in my eye. "Don't worry, this isn't your payment. You'll still get paid. You telling me you'll work for food just told me that you're desperate. I figure cash is the best tonic for desperation. This pie is my way of saying thank you to you. You made my wife happy."

I was stunned. Here was this mountain of a man who was grinning like a child because I gave him some berries. I tried the pie and it was delicious. "Wow," I said. "Your wife knows how to bake."

"You should try her cooking sometime," he said it before he realized it.

I smiled and accepted a coffee he handed to me and then went back to work. I had learned enough from the Thiessen's that workers and bosses didn't mix. I noticed I was the only Indian in the work crew and I knew that meant something. I didn't want to cross any more boundaries.

Days turned into weeks and the weather was beginning to turn colder. I enjoyed receiving two dollars at the end of each day and spent that money wisely but I was still sleeping outside.

"David!"

"Yes, sir."

"Come over here. I need to have a word with you."

"Yes, sir?"

"I want you to answer me truthfully. I've been watching you and you work hard. The men don't have anything bad to say about you, and you show up to work every day on time."

"Sir?"

"But I'm looking at things that they aren't. I'm going to guess that you aren't sleeping indoors, on account of you saving money?"

I looked down. I didn't say anything.

"I understand that things are tough. They are tough all over." He inhaled deeply. "Do you have family here?"

"Not in Winnipeg."

"But somewhere?"

"Back home, I've got a wife and three children. But it's too far from here."

He was quiet as he looked at me. I could feel his eyes cutting through my skin. "That must be tough for you."

"It is."

"Let me tell you what I'd like to do. It's something that may help you and me at the same time."

"OK..."

"I need someone to ensure that my site is secure. No kids smashing windows at night or starting fires. The normal stuff. The insurance company won't insure me unless someone is here. It isn't the Taj Mahal, but it will be dry and a lot warmer than sleeping outside."

"Do I need to pay for it?"

"No," he said. I could see him restraining a laugh. "I will pay you an extra dollar per night for you to stay. You will need to patrol the site at least twice per night but, otherwise, it should be an easy job."

"You'll pay me to stay inside your houses?"

"Just one room in one house," he added with the same glint in his eyes. His head looked to be twice the size of a normal man's head.

"Yes. Thank you, Mike." Part of me wanted to hug him but I rarely even hugged my family on the Res. I would never hug some big Ukrainian, however nice he was to me. I put my hand out and he unknowingly crushed it like before.

"You're welcome, David. There are a couple of rules. No parties, no guests. This is just for you." He gave my back a good slap and I went back to work.

I was set. I had a roof over my head and an income. Soon, I would have enough to bring Theresa down from the Res with our children.

✳

I wasn't promoted beyond shoveling dirt and sand and concrete. I began to learn about the other stages of construction but each stage had their own crew and they weren't interested in bringing me in. I didn't mind. I didn't need to think too much. I worked a full day and received a fair pay and then slept all night to earn another dollar. Pretty soon, I had saved enough money to start sending some back to Theresa. I wrote to her at least once a week and she would write back at least once a month. I knew she needed the money more than I did.

One month turned to one year, and then two. The leaves began falling in '34 when something inside me stirred. I had drunk alcohol before on the Res, even though it was a crime for an Indian to be in the possession of alcohol—on the Res or off. Since I left, I stayed off the stuff. But the days were long and the nights lonely without something to pass the time.

"Come on, David. Have a drink with us. It's a celebration!" Alice was holding a bottle of whiskey from its head and pouring it into any willing cup. The work day was over and the men were dispersing. The celebration was the birth of Mike's grandson. He brought over a case of whiskey for the men and said they had to drink it all but on one condition: that they didn't start until after work finished. I remember the cheer as all of us watched the clock until it struck five. I liked the way all of the men's faces lit up at the prospect.

"I can't. Thanks. Next time."

"Nonsense." She poured a large shot into my coffee cup. The bottle moved and I received an additional splash on my hand. She allowed herself to bump into me and I could smell the alcohol on her breath. I was glad she wasn't near an open flame or she'd have burst into fire.

She made her way around all the men, pulling out more whiskey as each bottle was drained. Somehow, she had become the barmaid for the party. Even Mike remained for a few toasts.

I smelled the whiskey mixed with my coffee. I put it to my lips and felt the warmth of the coffee and then the warmth of the liquor. It was a great combination and I didn't know why I hadn't had it before. I finished it at the same rate as the other men and took another shot, this time without the coffee.

When the men cleared the site, Alice remained. The weather was especially cold for the season and I invited Alice to finish the last bottle with me.

*
*

The next day, Mike was not pleased.

"David, you know the rules. I am not aware of you breaking them before this. But I can't have this."

"I'm sorry, Mike. It won't happen again."

"See to it that it doesn't." He knew what happened and probably blamed himself as much as me. I didn't want to disappoint him.

I went a week without a drink. Then, instead of sending money to Theresa, I bought some whiskey for myself. I drank it alone as I knew the rules. I didn't want to betray Mike's trust. I didn't need anyone to enjoy a drink. It went down easily and warmed me better than a blanket.

The next day, I felt weaker but still managed to do my job. It was hard work but it didn't need a lot of thought. That night, I had some more whiskey to ease the pain from the day. It helped relax me and I drank slowly until I fell asleep.

Each day, the work got harder and harder. Each night, the whiskey helped more and more. The pains would only go away after I had drunk at least a quarter of a bottle.

The first day I was late in two years, Mike pulled me aside.

"David, I can see you're going through a rough patch. I'm trying to be understanding but it's tough when it affects your work." His body hulked next to me. I could see the four layers of clothing he wore and the buttons that were unbuttoned to let it all breathe. I copied him but I was half his size.

"I'm sorry, Mike. It's just a little drink now and then. Sometimes I'm groggy when I wake up."

"Last warning, David. I don't want to do this, but my insurance won't cover any accidents if you are drunk or passed out and something happens. This is not a little matter."

"I understand," I said. I patted his shoulder and went to find my shovel. If I could have seen him, I would have seen sad eyes follow me; they looked as though they knew the path I was heading towards.

Within two weeks, I was fired. I lost my home and my job. Mike's eyes were watery as he handed me my final pay packet.

✻

I was back on the street and the snow had arrived. I had some money in my pocket, so I checked into the Occidental Hotel on Logan and Main. My room was basic but was better than sleeping outside. The music was loud and I wanted to see what all the commotion was all about.

"Double whiskey," I yelled above the music.

"You jusht booked in?" A toothless patron turned and began speaking at me. I looked over my shoulder before I realized he meant me.

"Yeah. Too cold to sleep outside."

He looked at me oddly. "You an Injun?"

I was annoyed. "Yeah. What about it?"

"Nothing, friend. Just ashking."

"What are you having?"

"Beer."

"Beer for my friend," I said. The barman nodded.

"Thanksh." He lifted his beer in a toast. "You know, there's easier ways than paying for it if all you wan is a warm place to shtay for the winter."

I looked at him and wasn't sure if I heard right. "What?"

"If you get yourself arrested, you can spend winter in jail. They feed you an it's warm and doesn't cosht anything."

"I don't want to be a criminal," I said. I turned my back and tried to watch the band playing. The bar was packed.

"You're already a criminal," he said. "You're an Injun. They won treat you any different. At leasht you won die in the cold when your money runs out."

I tried to ignore him. "Another, please." The barman nodded and put another double in front of me. I put it down and circled my fingers for another round. He nodded and obliged. I put it down and ordered a beer.

The music became more indistinct and I no longer heard the drunk next to me. I didn't notice what time it was when a fight broke out three paces from me. I picked up my drink so it wouldn't spill and tried to get out of the way of the bodies. The bouncers ran in and tried to break it up. Someone pulled a knife and, suddenly, there was blood everywhere. The band stopped and the lights went on. The fight had spread and it looked like at least ten guys were going at it. I inched my way towards the exit and left with my beer. I didn't want to get caught up in any of that.

"You! Stop!" The voice was loud and came from a big man in a round hat. I realized it was the RCMP. I'd had run-ins with them back on the Res. I stopped in my tracks.

"Yes, sir. I'm just trying to avoid the fight going on in there."

The normal police already passed me and had gone into the hotel's bar entrance. I was alone with the big RCMP guy. He must have been waiting for someone because he turned and looked down Main Street. I didn't see anything other than an odd horse and the skeletal overhead lines of the trams. He was the same height and size as Mike, my old boss. He had a full moustache and a stick that hung from his hip.

I finished my beer in the cold. I could see my breath and I watched him out of the corner of my eye.

"Do you have any identification papers on you?" His voice was directed at me again.

"No, sir."

"You know that it is against the law for an Indian to be in the possession of alcohol?"

"I am not in possession of any alcohol, sir." It was true. I had drunk it all.

He stepped closer to me. "Now don't you start giving me any trouble, boy, or you'll be sorry you even–"

His words were cut short as I smashed my beer bottle against his head. The rest happened like it was a dream. I saw him close his eyes and absorb the hit. When his eyes opened, I felt like a mouse in an eagle's talons. He grabbed me by the neck and threw me to the ground. I felt the first kick in my ribs. There was a second kick in the same place. I heard the sound of his stick against my legs and then head. The rest I learned when I woke up two days later.

※

"You're lucky, son. We weren't sure if you were going to come out of it."

"Wha?" I was lying down and the room was all in white. I was in pain but I also couldn't move.

"Don't struggle. You're strapped in."

"Where am I?"

"You're in the infirmary."

"Where?"

"A hospital. You've been charged with assaulting an RCMP constable. That's a serious crime. You'll do time for that."

"And my injuries?"

"He claims it was self-defence. His face is badly cut up. Before we get into that, what's your name?"

"David."

"Do you have a last name?"

"Bass. David Bass."

"OK, David. This is what is going to happen. You will recuperate here until you are fit enough to go to jail. There'll be a trial, but I wouldn't hold your breath. When you are in jail, try not to get into any trouble or else I'll be patching you up again. Understand?"

My head was killing me. I nodded and it felt like I had rocks rolling in my skull.

"Good. Behave, and you'll be out by the summer."

Remember Who You Are

"This has to be the worst-smelling place in Winnipeg." Frank Burns was tall and wiry with an anchor tattooed on his left forearm with four aces behind it.

"It's not too bad," I said.

"Compared to what?"

"At least it's a job."

"You don't expect much of yourself do you, David?"

"I've spent too much time in jail and on the street. I earn enough for three square meals and a place to sleep."

"And you stink like it." His yellow-stained teeth grinned at me.

I shrugged. "I guess it's true about a donkey."

"What's that?"

"He doesn't smell his own crap."

Frank laughed at that and poked the soaking furs. "I hear they're thinking of shutting this place down."

"I wouldn't believe it," I said. "Too many people buy these furs. My people depend on these furs."

"Your people. What do they do other than get drunk and live off the taxpayer?" He was smiling but there was nothing friendly about his words.

I didn't say anything against him. Instead, I changed the subject. "The Hudson's Bay Company won't let places like this go under."

"You think they can keep a whole industry alive?"

"Not every business is going under. They say demand is finally increasing in Europe, and the U.S. is starting to improve."

"Now the Indian knows business, too?" Frank had lost his smile and began berating me. I didn't understand why he did this. Maybe he drank on the job or had a fight with his wife. I knew he wouldn't change, so I didn't bother getting angry at him.

"I'm going to the prep area," I said instead.

The tannery was located just past St. Boniface, the French quarter in Winnipeg. I got out of jail in the spring of '35 and found the job shortly after. At first, I vomited at the smells. Then, I realized it was the continuation of the work my people did in the bush—thousands of trappers and hunters who skinned animals and traded with the Hudson's Bay Company. They ate the meat and fed their communities and sold the fur. I could always tell a quality trapper or hunter by the way the flesh was cleaned off the skin. After three years, I have been involved in all the elements of cleaning, stretching, curing, treating and making of leather and furs that people wear every day.

I never realized the number of processes necessary to get the hard piece of pelt that I had seen in the wild to the supple coat that people wore. Back home, the women dealt with this and I wasn't interested in learning. I started at the bottom, putting the hard pelts in the solution to make them soft. I worked up to the point of thinning down the swollen leather with a spinning blade called a flesher's knife. It was scary and my wages got docked when I cut through the leather. It was scarier when they told me I had to learn every stage in the process. I liked the oiling of the leather and final stages. I never understood how the fur stayed looking so good after being soaked in chemicals and covered with sawdust. It was then hung, cut and shaped. In some way, I saw the furs as an example of me. The truth of the material survived everything. In the end, the beaver or mink fur comes out looking like a million bucks. I just hoped I would come out the same way, in time.

I was sending money to Theresa again and received the occasional postcard in return. I stayed away from the whiskey and beer and tried to live life in a way that would make my children proud. It didn't help that I was so lonely and that I had to work with such nasty people.

"You care about what's going on in Europe?" Frank asked.

"Only as long as it doesn't affect my job," I said.

"Don't you read the papers?"

"Would it make a difference?"

"You Indians are a funny lot. Are you even Canadian?"

The question made me think. I didn't say anything. I was hanging the pelts, leather up, on the wooden dowels to let the sawdust and chemical fall off naturally. We had a large batch of beaver that needed to be processed.

"I mean, if there's war, will you fight?"

"My father went to the First World War. He even got a medal."

"Wow. I didn't know." He seemed genuinely impressed. I was surprised to see his hard exterior soften. I wasn't sure if it was respect or surprise.

"He was a scout. He doesn't talk about it to me."

"Same as all the vets. They prefer to get drunk and tell each other their stories. Same as my dad."

I was even more surprised at this. We had worked together for three years and he would alternate from being friendly to being a proper sonofabitch. He had never mentioned his father before to me. I kept silent and moved the pelts onto their wooden dowels. I couldn't afford to lose this job. The boss let me sleep in one of the empty rooms. It helped me a lot and allowed me to send more money back home.

"David! Post for you." The voice was Edna, a large watery woman who had a nice smile and never said a bad word about anyone, including me.

"Thanks. I'll pick it up on my break."

"Another love letter from your missus?" Frank said. His eyes had a different look in them now.

"Probably. It's been a while, and I don't get post from anyone else." I was excited but didn't want to show it. Every beaver became a nuisance as I willed the time to move faster.

My break finally arrived and I went to Edna to retrieve my post. There was only one letter. I was hoping for a parcel of food or some pictures or keepsake. I put it in my pocket. I would read it after work.

The rest of the day passed slowly as the letter burned a warm reminder in my breast pocket. When the last of the pelts were stamped and tagged, I washed up and went upstairs and to the end of the hallway where my room was. I had a bed, a small table and a chair. It wasn't much but it was warm, safe and secure. And I never had to worry about being late for work.

I opened the letter and noticed that the writing was in a different hand than Theresa's. I immediately became concerned that something may have happened to her. It read:

Dear David:

I'm glad to see you are firmly on your feet. These last eight years have been hard on both of us. I can only imagine how lonely you have been. I have also been lonely and I missed you terribly, as have the children.

Your money has been put to good use and we are all well.

You may have noticed that this is not my handwriting. It is my sister's. I couldn't write this letter as my hand shook too much. You have been gone so long, I forget what you look like. I hope our son will be in your image. I'm told by your family that he is.

I could feel tears fill my eyes and I felt like returning home right then. It wasn't fair on Theresa or the children for me to be away for so long.

So what I am about to write pains me more than you can know. I was lonely and I have found a man. We have three children together. I was going to wait until you returned and beg your forgiveness but I realize now that you should hear this before deciding to return.

What? I re-read the letter to that point in case I missed something. How could she not tell me? How could my parents not tell me? Was I dead to them? Tears began to fall.

I know you may never forgive what I have done. I am happy and I hope you can find it in your heart to be happy for us.

I will always love you, David.

Theresa

I slumped against the wall, not noticing that my body slid until I was sitting on the ground. The letter lay in my hands and I re-read it a dozen times to ensure I was understanding what I thought it said.

After an hour of sitting, I got up and put the letter with the others I had received until now. I put on my coat and walked outside. I walked until I found a shop prepared to sell me a bottle of whiskey. I bought two, just in case. I returned to my room and began to drink.

The first touch of the whiskey to my lips was like an old friend coming home. I didn't rush it. I sipped slowly, allowing it to cover my tongue and warm my throat. I felt its effects after the fourth large drink. After that, my body began to become numb and I forgot about Theresa and her letter and my three children and her three new children. I tried to push the thoughts out of my mind that, while I was in prison, she found a new man.

I drank until the questions stopped being asked by my brain. "Why didn't she tell me before? Why didn't anyone tell me before? Do I mean so little to everyone that I am not entitled to the truth?"

I drank until my eyes struggled to stay open. My breathing became heavy as I slumped against the wall, sitting on my bed.

I drank until my lips and tongue and body couldn't distinguish water from air. My mouth opened and closed. I poured some more in. I swallowed. I tried to open my eyes but they preferred to stay shut. I swung my legs onto the bed and felt my head become heavy. I put my glass down next to the empty bottle and decided to rest for a minute before the next drink.

*
*

It was Frank who found me.

"David, get up. Come on. Stop messing around."

"Hmm." I could feel my lungs fill and empty. My eyes still refused to open. I could hear my breathing through my nose and felt a pain grip my head. My muscles were sore and I needed to sleep.

"The boss is here, David. You need to get moving."

"I can't."

"You have to. Here, I've got coffee. If you get moving now, I'll be able to cover for you. But you need to get down there. He'll notice."

I yawned like a dog, with my tongue curling upwards. My eyes were still closed and I swung my legs off the bed. I couldn't remember feeling so sore and so tired. He put a cup of coffee in my hand. I managed to open one eye and saw the steam rising from it. I also saw the look of concern on Frank's face.

"I'll be OK," I lied.

"You don't look OK. Hey, I read your letter. I'm sorry as hell over that. No man should have that hand dealt to him."

I didn't understand why he was being so kind. I decided I would never understand Frank.

"Finish your coffee and splash some water on your face. I'll be back."

I watched him leave and finished the coffee before laying down on the bed. It felt so comfortable. I figured I'd just close my eyes for ten more minutes. I'll feel better then.

"David!"

"Huh? I'm up. I'm getting up." My eyes were shut and I sat on the edge of the bed breathing heavily, willing myself to put my feet on the floor and stand up.

"Don't bother. You're fired."

I heard the words and one of my eyes opened long enough to see my boss shaking his head as he stomped out of my room.

"David, wake up." It was Frank again.

"Why bother?" I said. "I'm already fired. What else are they going to do to me?"

"Maybe jail? Don't you remember what you did?"

The 'J' word gave me a jolt. Both eyes opened. I tried hard to focus. "What? I've been here drinking. So what if I'm late for one day of work? I shouldn't be fired for that."

I saw Frank look at me from the side of his eyes. "Then you don't remember." He paced the room. He had a genuinely worried look on his face. "You don't remember trashing the place? I was able to salvage the pelts and I hid the ones that were cut. If he were to find those, you'd definitely end up in jail."

I shook my head. "I swear. I've been here the whole time." I looked over and saw both bottles of whiskey had been drunk. I thought I had only drunk one. I saw what looked like vomit on the floor next to my bed. I looked down and realized that I had soiled myself as well.

"You have no memory of what you did?" Frank was looking at me with astonishment.

I was beginning to become afraid of what I did. "None."

"Then perhaps the best thing would be for you to gather your things and try to disappear before anything more is discovered." He had his hand on my shoulder. I felt as though he had seen this before and was worried. I still didn't understand why.

"OK. I'll be out of here as soon as I can."

✳

The next thing I remember was waking up here. I could feel my face bruised and the world was sideways. Then I realized I was lying on my side on the street. The sun was up and I was somewhere between two large brick buildings. There was stone on the lower six feet of the buildings and red brick on the rest. I must be in a back alley. I could smell the garbage. Or that could be me. I couldn't care less.

I found a bottle in my jacket pocket and took another drink. It helped with the pain. I couldn't move at first. I saw a large crow standing on the garbage cans next to me, about ten feet away. It was cawing.

My jacket was still in one piece only because it was quality leather. My pants were torn and I wished all my clothes were leather. At least my boots were still on me. I looked at the bird and realized it wasn't a crow. It was a raven.

"What are you doing here, in town?" I asked it.

"Looking for you," it said.

I shook myself and became afraid. "Birds don't talk," I said.

"I'm not a bird."

"Then what are you?"

"Don't you recognize me?"

I tried to focus but the pain in my head and the effects of the whiskey made that impossible. "No. Who are you?"

"I'm your friend. Don't you remember me?"

I saw the raven's beak opening and closing. I didn't understand how the words were getting to my head.

I shook my head. "I'm sorry."

"What's your name?"

"David," I said.

"No. Your real name."

"Da–." I paused. I had almost forgotten. "Migizi."

"That's right, my friend. You are Migizi and I am?"

"I don't know."

"I had a shadow that protected me."

I became cold with the memory.

"You protected me the best you could."

I began to shake.

"You saw me and I saw you. I told you I'd look out for you."

I began to cry.

"l will always be here for you. But you need to remember who you are."

"I don't remember," I cried. I had sat up to look at the raven. It continued in its deep throaty *'kraa'* and I continued to hear Geezis' voice.

"You will. Seek yourself. Find yourself. Become who you are meant to be."

I hung my head in shame at what I had become. For two years after getting fired from the tannery, I allowed myself to wallow in despair and fear, no longer working or caring. All I wanted was for the pain to go away.

When I looked up, the raven was gone. I pulled myself to my feet and threw the remains of my whiskey into the garbage.

"I will find you again, Geezis."

*
*

I went to the Salvation Army soup kitchen and got some food. World War II had broken out over a year ago and this was the only place I could find that still gave free food. I agreed to listen to their version of mass and was allowed to sleep inside. Perhaps my prayers were answered, because I overheard some Indians, talking Ojibwe, two cots away from me. I didn't say anything but I listened. What I learned became my next destination. I began walking towards it the next day.

Five days later, I reached Pine Falls and found what I was looking for: a reserve that practiced Indian medicine illegally. I knew that all Indian medicine was as illegal as me possessing alcohol. But as I had become a drunk, I also knew that some things still happened regardless of whether they were legal or not.

I put one foot in front of the other and walked towards the houses I saw in the distance. I had no idea who I needed to see. I just knew I needed to be there and someone there would be able to help me.

"Are you looking for someone?" The voice came from my left.

"Hello? Hi, I am looking for someone who can help me," I said. It was vague but I didn't know how to ask for help.

He was a little shorter than me and a lot fatter. As he was an elder, I didn't want to offend. I remembered that much from my past.

"Help for what?" His voice was calm. His face was clear of strain. His hair was long, pulled back with a leather string at the back.

I paused, embarrassed. "I need help remembering."

He raised his eyebrow. "I don't know if we can help with that. But let's start by getting to know each other. What's your name?"

"David," I said. Then I corrected myself. "My name is Migizi."

He smiled. "Nice to meet you, Migizi. That is a strong name. My name is Shkaabewis. It means helper to the medicine people. Do you know what your name means?"

"No."

"The eagle. The most powerful and majestic of all the birds. You have greatness in you, Migizi."

"I don't feel so great."

"That is a good first step."

I didn't know what Shkaabewis meant, but I followed him.

"I wait for spirits like yours to find us," he said. "We live in difficult times and it is easy to forget who we are."

I remained silent and followed him. He was so calm. His belly was large and I felt small next to him.

"Have you ever been in a sweat lodge?"

"No. What is it?"

He shook his head. "I will show you. But first, we pray." He showed me into a dome-like tent where he sat down. He indicated for me to do the same. I did. As we walked, I noticed other people watching me from their doors and windows. No one joined us.

"I don't have anything to give you," I said.

He smiled and put his hand on my arm. "Don't worry about any of that now. Here. Take this and put it in your left hand and hold it near your heart."

I took some yellowed leaves and held them as he instructed.

"Pray with me," he said. He then began to speak in the language I had all but forgotten. The language of my Ojibwe people—soft, like the rustling of wind or the sound of rain against the earth.

I could feel myself begin to sway. He stopped speaking and had made a small fire in the middle of the tent.

"Pass the tobacco from your left hand to your right. Good. Now release it into the fire. Gently. Good. Now relax."

He got up and left briefly before returning with four more elders. They each nodded and took a seat around the fire. He took what looked like a small frying pan and used tongs to take some coals from the fire. He then took what looked like a bundle of weeds and placed it on top of the coals. It began to smoke. He blew lightly on the coals to increase the heat.

Shkaabewis then walked to each of the elders and held the smoking mixture in front of them. Each elder wafted their hands over the smoke, bringing it towards them as though washing in it. They covered their head, face, and then chest and rubbed their hands together as if it had been water cleansing them.

When it came to me, he indicated me to copy what the elders had done. He then walked around me and used his own hands to waft it onto me, my back, and even my feet. He wafted some more onto my face and told me to inhale a little and rub it into my ears and face. When everyone had finished, he sat down and did the same to himself.

One of the elders began to speak. I didn't know if it was a prayer or a speech. It was the same Ojibwe language that gently caressed me like the sage smoke.

We sat like that for a number of hours, each elder taking turns. I was silent and allowed the healing to begin. When I heard the crackling of the cedar in the fire, I looked towards Shkaabewis and he smiled in reply. "The crackling calls the spirits," he said. He became calm as did the others.

Outside, I began to hear the sounds of a drum. It was soft at first. My body shuddered as I first heard the drums when Geezis died.

"It is the heartbeat of Earth," Shkaabewis said. I don't know how he could see me amidst all the smoke. "Embrace the heartbeat of our creator."

I felt the drums as much as heard them.

✳

I stayed with Shkaabewis at their reserve for another two years while I healed.

When I decided to join the war effort like my father before me, I went into Winnipeg and found a recruitment office. When the recruiting officer asked what my name was, I didn't hesitate.

"Migizi."

CHAPTER
EIGHT

Finding Purpose

"**G**eezer!"

"Yes, sir!"

"Don't call me 'sir'. I work for a living."

"Sorry, Sergeant."

"I'm not looking to French-kiss you, son. Just look lively."

I stood at attention. I wasn't going to try and get the last word in with the sergeant.

"I want to see you put a hole in that target."

"Which number, Sergeant?" My reply was spoken in three sharp barks, my stomach tightening with each word. I focused my eyes dead ahead of me.

"Number five."

I turned to look down range. It looked to be a former gravel pit. The sides were high and all around us. On the ground was a row of sandbags to rest a rifle on. There were eight of us with rifles. The rest were instructors and the sergeant. Number five target was set at six hundred yards. I knew this because I had already shot this target yesterday.

Prior to joining the army, I had shot my father's gun when hunting deer and smaller game. I preferred to fish and trap but my father wanted me to know how to track and kill large game. It was part of who we were, he told me. I didn't understand how killing something defenceless could be a good thing, but he told me the deer was a gift to us and we would respect it by eating its flesh and using its pelt. I did what I was told, but it gave me no pleasure. That was before I joined the army and before I felt the Lee-Enfield .303 in my hands.

The Lee-Enfield was the standard rifle issued by the British Army. Canada, being a faithful colony, followed suit. I loved the weight of it and the accuracy of it in my hands. It was as though I was born to use this tool. I didn't think about what I would be shooting if I ever came into contact with the enemy. I was enjoying being good at something. I saw the respect the other soldiers had in their eyes when they looked at me. Amazingly, even the Sergeant with his gruff manner found himself swearing under his breath after I shot. I realized later that this was his version of a compliment.

I put the rifle in position and lay down next to it. I put the butt of the gun into my shoulder and rolled my head once before aligning the sights with my target. I exhaled and pulled the trigger at the magical moment when the lungs are empty but not beginning to fill. I did not hold my breath or alter any of my normal functions. I let the gun become an extension of my eyes. I could feel the weight of the bullet and the distance it needed to travel. I instinctively knew how high to adjust the barrel. Everything was open sights and the rifle had a mechanism that would flip up to help calculate the distances. I never used it. I felt the wind and the target and willed the bullet to meet it. I could never explain why it worked for me or how.

"Geezer!" He slapped me on my helmet. "Do it again."

I did.

Only the Sergeant was making any sound. Then he squatted next to me and began tapping repeatedly on my helmet. "Do it again," he said. He didn't stop tapping my helmet.

I did.

"Again."

I did.

"Cease firing. At ease, soldier."

I made sure the gun was unloaded and the chamber clear. I stood up and slung the rifle on my shoulder.

"That was some fine shooting, Geezer."

"Thank you, Sergeant." It was the greatest compliment any of us had ever heard pass his lips. I noticed the faces on the others. They were all nodding in unison. I had never felt prouder in my life.

He turned his attention to Paddy and I went to mingle with the others. Each one made sure to pat my shoulder or back and say how well I had shot. I knew I was a good shot, but it was always good to feel the love from your colleagues. If I was going to war with them, we would all live or die as brothers. We all had to endure the target practice, with the Sergeant tapping our helmets and yelling in our ear. When we left, he pulled me aside.

"Geezer, I'd like a word with you." His voice was gravelly from smoking and yelling. I had never heard his voice at a conversational level. It seemed odd, almost friendly.

"Yes, Sergeant?"

"I have been tasked with supplying some recruits to an experimental force. It is dangerous. They need soldiers who are used to the cold and who can survive as individuals while still working as a team. I would like to submit your name."

"Thank you, Sergeant."

"Don't thank me. From what I understand, it'll make your basic training here feel like a walk in the park. You need to volunteer for this. If you're agreeable, I'll tell them you volunteered."

"Thank you, Sergeant. I won't let you down." I thought I was feeling pride earlier, but this was even better. My toes and fingers tingled and I felt a warm jolt of heat shoot through my torso. I was shocked when he extended his hand and shook mine. He turned and left. I followed in a daze.

*

I had been on a train before, but not across all of Canada and definitely never into the United States. By the time I crossed the border, I was part of a large number of fellow soldiers, probably two or three hundred. They made us change over to train carriages with the windows painted black. We travelled for a long time like that. I liked it. It meant we were doing something top secret.

"Grab your bags, gentlemen. You have reached your destination." A porter walked briskly through the carriages, repeating himself every few rows. He was smiling and his face was flush. I didn't hear him slur his words.

I followed my fellow soldiers out of the train and into busses that took us for another two hours' drive. The destination looked worse than any reserve I had seen. There were a few wooden structures but I assumed those were for officers and the instructors. I noticed some tents and began walking in that direction. I was right. I was grouped with five other soldiers from Canada and our first instruction was to make our accommodation.

"Do any of you know what this is all about?" One of my new tent-mates was the first amongst us to break the silence.

"No," another answered. I still had no idea who they were or what their names were. I could read their names and rank on their uniform, but no one worth their salt went by those names. We were all given nicknames.

"I was told they're forming a special para unit." This was from someone with a Scottish accent. I was always amazed when I understood him. He spoke a very different English from the one I did.

"Jumping from planes?" I asked. I hadn't heard anything about this. "I've never even been on a plane before."

"Me neither," the Scottish accent replied. "But they sent me here anyway. Perhaps they know what they want."

I kept my head down and concentrated on getting the base for the tent in place. We all worked well together. "At least it's not raining," I said. I wanted to say something to break the silence.

"Amen to that. By the way, I'm Lewis Bain. My friends call me Scotty." I barely understood what he said in his Scottish accent and was pleased with his nickname.

"Mine's Geezer," I said.

The others laughed. "Nice one," a few of them said.

"I'm Logan Gagnon. My friends call me Caz."

"What's that short for?"

"They seem to envy my influence with the ladies," Caz smiled.

"Casanova?" Scotty asked. We all laughed, but I think it was at the way he pronounced Casanova. He made it sound like a pet name for his cow rather than a famous lover.

The others were Scott Brown (aka 'Tunes'), Ken Clark (aka 'Superman') and Kirk Campbell who didn't have a nickname. Scotty suggested calling Kirk No-name, but I didn't think it would stick.

It was good to have people to talk to while we worked. I didn't make any friends on the train. I didn't want to look weak, so I didn't speak. This felt good, like old times on Thiessen's farm or with Geezis. I felt a shadow pass over me as those memories entered my mind. I shook my head and allowed the warm July sun to wash away the hurt.

We each set up our beds and made ourselves at home. By the time evening was up, we were ready for a well-deserved sleep. We knew that next morning started at 04:30. We were warned that they were only looking for the best. I was beginning to believe that I could be one of those lucky few.

Morning came faster than I thought. I felt a boot in my ribcage and watched my tent-mates get the same treatment.

"Everyone up. Get yourselves shit-showered-shaved-and-changed and on the square. If you want to eat, you need to go via the square." He was gone before I could digest what he was saying. All I heard was "eat square shit." I knew that couldn't be right.

I rolled out and made myself ready. There was hot water and I had the best shower for a long time. I shaved what little facial hair I had in the shower and scrubbed my hair clean. I wanted to be part of this new group. When they looked at me, they saw a man with skills they needed. I put on the issued khaki pants and stopped to admire the insignia. It was in the shape of a red arrowhead with USA printed horizontally on top and Canada printed vertically. I traced its outline with my fingers.

"All right, gentlemen," the US Staff Sergeant bellowed in front of us. "You know you are tough. Otherwise, you wouldn't be here. You know you have skills. You wouldn't have been recommended without that. And I hope you know that you're all a little crazy—otherwise you wouldn't have volunteered."

I felt myself wanting to smile. I could hear a few chuckles from down the line but I didn't turn my face. I knew they were watching us. I also knew that drill sergeants were bred to be mean to their charges and he just gave us a compliment. It meant he was now probably going to hurt us and try to break us and only the toughest would survive. Each minute I stood there I felt as though this unit was designed for me. I had been through more than any of these other soldiers and I was still alive. I was unbreakable.

"...and the most important thing you need to remember," he said, "is to keep on top of your injuries. If you are injured, you go home. If you cannot complete an exercise, you go home. If God strikes your tent with lightning and you are ten minutes late, you go home. There are no excuses. There are no exceptions." He went silent and put his eyes on each one of ours. When his met mine, I could feel the electricity of a predator meeting another killer. It did something to me. My body began to change in reply.

He talked some more and tried to scare us but I could sense that none of the men were concerned. We broke for breakfast at 06:30 and sat in awe at the quality of the food in front of us.

"This is better than any restaurant I've been to," Scotty said. Lacking any other grouping, we sat by tent.

"That doesn't say much," Caz said. When he ate his eggs and bacon, he began to nod. "I take it back. This is incredible."

I took a bite. The mess trays were standard military stainless steel but the food on it was the best I've eaten for as long as I could remember. "I'm beginning to feel like a turkey," I said.

"Why?"

"I'm being fattened up for the slaughter."

That got a few chuckles. The entire mess hall was quiet as the food was consumed. All I could hear was the sound of metal on metal as the forks and knives and spoons touched the trays. The talking only started up again when the coffee was served and full bodies sat back in appreciation.

The rest of the day was a blur. We were no longer allowed to walk. We marched double time between exercises. We ran an evil obstacle course at 08:00 and then ran until our bodies screamed for rest. I heard that sixty mile marches were going to be regular events as part of our conditioning. We met our hand-to-hand combat instructor. He was an ex-Shanghai International Police Officer named Pat O'Neill. I liked him. He reminded me of my uncle. We were shown the weapons we were going to use. We were also told that we would become proficient with the enemy's weapons. It was like going to a candy store and trying to take in everything at once.

Before I knew it, we were sleeping and waiting for day two.

Day two started the same way. This time we met our Commanding Officer, Colonel Robert Frederick. If he had a nickname, we didn't know it.

"Gentlemen, today you will jump from a plane. Now is the time to quit if you can't handle that. If you don't complete your jump, you will go home." He paused to take in our faces. There was a small smirk on his face. He began to pace the space along the front of our assembly. "There is nothing to fear once you are trained. You are all here to be trained. You are not participating in a sport. You are learning how to kill. We will help mould you into the ultimate hunter killers capable of surviving any terrain, attacking under any circumstance and projecting your will over any opposition. That is our purpose here." He began to pace alongside the perimeter of the assembly to get a closer look at the soldiers in the back.

"It is all about patience, silence, and sudden violence. It is about acting as one with the force of many. You are the chosen few who may become members of the 1st Special Service Force. Our objective is to be better, stronger, and faster than our enemy. We plan, recon, assault, and extract. When you are called to action, you are not there to talk to the enemy. You are there to harass, kill, and humiliate them."

I couldn't help it. I began to grin. I knew I was going to get disciplined for it. I didn't move my head and willed my smile away.

"My job is to train you. I will ask nothing of you I won't do myself. And part of this is to eat well. I have pulled every string in this army to get you the best food. I have standing orders with the cooks to buy the best. If that isn't possible, we'll steal it. I'll do my part. The rest is up to you."

He nodded to the staff sergeant and left the square. The sergeant began hollering at us but I couldn't hear what he said. The words of the colonel were ringing in my ears. The idea of jumping out of a plane wasn't something I would choose to do, but there was no way I wasn't jumping out of that plane now. I just hoped that all that good food would stay inside me when I did.

In the end, we didn't need to find a nickname for Kirk Campbell. He broke his leg on the first jump and he had to go. Only Scotty, Caz and I managed to stick it out over the six months. Tunes couldn't get the hang of skiing and was sent home for no other reason. Superman didn't live up to his name and couldn't handle the sheer rock face we were all forced to climb.

✳
✳

By the time we finished our conditioning, we believed we were the best fighting force on the planet and were looking forward to making contact with an enemy to prove it. In July, 1943, they sent us out to the Aleutian Islands, somewhere west of Alaska. The Japs had taken the islands and the

Americans were mad as hell. I felt a strange pride when I found out the only other foreign military power to occupy parts of the United States was Canada in 1812. We invaded on August 15th but the Japs had already abandoned the island and we were redeployed stateside.

"Do you think this time we'll see some action?" Caz sat next to me as we approached Naples. Many of the other men were sick but I enjoyed the constant movement of the boat.

"I hope so," I said. "It'd be a waste of training if we didn't."

"I don't think they're making us fight like the rest of them," Scotty said. By now, I had learned to understand his accent.

"Whad'ya mean?"

"Don't you remember what the colonel told us? We not going to slug it out face to face World War I style. We are tasked with fighting dirty. We are here to get the job done and to harass the enemy."

"And leave our calling card," I smiled.

"I like that part," Caz said. "Cocky as hell. Colonel Frederick is one tricky sonofabitch."

The soldiers next to us heard Caz's last few words and all began nodding and smiling and giving each other slaps on the back. We were all smoking.

Naples was nothing like I expected. The Mediterranean was beautiful as it met the beaches and the earth rose up with its cities and trees beyond. I can't remember the name of the place we docked. We were a mass of bodies and I followed my CO's commands. We walked into and through Naples and joined the US 36th Infantry Division. I was struck by the beautiful women who appeared amidst the rubble as we walked. I couldn't accept the food they offered as I knew they were starving compared to me. Some of the other soldiers accepted the food because it came with a kiss. We hadn't fired one shot but we had brought hope to the people.

"So this is the mission we've been training for?" Scotty said.

"I don't know," I said. "I thought we were going to Norway. They sent us, instead, to the middle of nowhere in the Pacific. Now we're in Italy."

"'Cause we're the best, my friend." Caz had a crazy smile on his face. He was accepting the kisses along with the wine. I think he was a bit drunk.

"Do you know where we're going?" I asked.

"No," Caz said. "But it looks serious."

"The rubble in Naples looks serious," I said. "I've never seen anything like it."

"That's because you've never left Manitoba before, my friend."

I laughed along partly because it was true. I hadn't been anywhere. The army had taken me in and provided me structure. The one thing that struck me most was that it treated me like a man and not an Indian. For that, I was prepared to shed blood. And here I was, about to do just that.

On December 1, 1943, we were all trucked within six miles of the base of a strategic mountain called Monte la Difensa. The Germans had a force of men and artillery on the top. They controlled everything as far as could be seen. It was impossible to liberate Italy without that mountaintop. As part of the 2nd Regiment, I would scale the mountain at night and attack at dawn. At 16:30 hours, we began the six-mile march to take us to the beginning of the ascent.

"They know we're coming," I said as quietly as possible to Caz who marched in front of me.

"You think?" While I couldn't see his face, I could imagine his smirk. In front of us, the entire mountain was being shelled. Bursts of flame and explosions were everywhere.

"If you were wondering what hell looks like boys, it's right in front of you." Scotty was behind and I could hear the fear in his voice. Hell, I was afraid but

I wouldn't be the one to back down. It had begun to rain and it wasn't looking like it would stop.

"Someone has ratted us out," I said.

"Can't do much about that now," Caz replied. "We live or die on what we do now. Remember what O'Neil said."

"We're never going to get close enough for hand-to-hand with those bastards," I said.

"Not that. I'm talking about closing in on your enemy when he least expects it. Right now, the Krauts are shelling the crap out of us. They hope we are on the mountain and that they are blowing us to bits. They expect us to retreat and regroup. Instead, we'll scale that mountain at night when they are tucked in bed and destroy them in the morning."

"They're sleeping soundly because they know it's suicide to climb the face of the mountain," I said. "Especially in this rain."

"Suicide for mere mortals. Not the 1st Special Service Force." Scotty had come up next to me and joined the conversation.

"I'm with you guys," I said. "But I'd be lying if I said this was going to be easy."

"Easy is for wimps," Scotty grinned. I couldn't help myself. Both he and Caz were crazy. Perhaps I was a bit crazy myself. Marching into artillery fire was not my idea of fun but I would gladly do it again for those two.

By midnight, we had reached the most dangerous position. We were one thousand feet below the Germans and within easy killing range–if they knew we were there. Our only hope was silence and the element of surprise. Perhaps the rain gave the Germans comfort that no one would attempt anything in those conditions.

I looked at the impossibly flat rock that extended forever above us. When I looked back at Caz and Scotty, all I saw was determination. It steeled me and I began to climb. I was one of the best climbers in the regiment so it was up to me to make the foray and secure ropes for the others. It felt suicidal. I gripped with every fibre of my body. At some points, only my fingernails held me from falling to my death. Where I could get a foothold, I anchored my ropes. I began to feel better as the anchors increased and the distance between me and the enemy decreased. By the time I reached the top, I had torn three finger nails almost completely off; the blood was beginning to give me trouble. I patched myself up the best I could. I knew the swelling would make it difficult to fire on the enemy if it got worse.

There were six hundred men in our regiment and we needed to lift our weapons, water and bodies up one thousand feet. We knew that as soon as it was dawn, we were all dead if we weren't in position. I couldn't think beyond getting our men off the cliff side and onto the small depression where we would make our assault against the German entrenchment.

When all the men were up, we took a breather. We sat soaked in our own sweat and the incessant rain. It must have been 04:00 and none of us could believe we had made it up. None of us talked. We knew that talking or even coughing would alert the enemy.

The plan was to attack at 06:00 and the men began to prepare their weapons. Each rifle was carefully handled to ensure no banging against other metal. My own rifle was the US government issued M1 Garand .30-06. I loved it better than my Canadian Lee-Enfield .303. I felt strangely protective of the rifle's wood and oiled metal against the rain. Like everyone else, I had a condom secured on the end to ensure no rain or dirt got inside the barrel itself.

My muscles ached and I was tired from the adrenaline rush of nearly dying on the climb. I settled against the hard, disinterested stone and tried to sleep until the appointed time. Caz and Scotty crouched next to me and found their own stone pillows. No one spoke. No one slept.

Our CO, Lt. Col. Mac William, gave his orders in hand signals. We were told to take up positions. All six hundred of us began to reposition ourselves. My body wanted to sleep. It needed ten minutes of sleep. It wanted hours. It got nothing.

The next thing I saw was the sky alight in flares. Our men began the assault immediately. We caught the Germans off-guard and with their guns pointing in the wrong direction. We inflicted heavy casualties on them. I remember taking a shot and watching the impact of my bullet go through a machine gunner's helmet. His body fell away and his gun fell silent.

But these were war-hardened soldiers who had seen action in Russia. They were the 104th Panzergrenadier Division and the Hermann Göering Paratrooper Division. Their names alone generated fear amongst many in the Allied forces. And we were within seventy-five feet of them, exchanging small arms fire.

I heard the distinctive rapid fire of the Thompson machine gun next to me. Caz had opened up on the enemy and was screaming something. Nothing could be heard. We all acted on instinct and training.

Mortars were fired at them and at us. I threw all my grenades at them. I kept reminding myself to conserve my ammunition.

I threw myself behind a rock as the Germans returned fire. They were as good as us, I thought. Well, almost.

I looked at our blackened faces. We went in at night because night was the killing time. In the flashes, I could see their white faces scream with anger and terror. They knew it was over but were fighting to the death.

I saw my fellow soldiers die within inches of me. It was fast. One moment they were there, firing and running alongside me, and the next moment they were on the ground. Usually the wound was unseen at first. Sometimes it was obvious—when a mortar round would turn them into hamburger. I looked at the bodies and realized it could be me lying there. Instead of fear, I felt rage. I took my fallen friends' ammunition and used it to fell the enemy.

I lost track of Caz and Scotty and focussed on flanking the enemy and putting bullets into them. As I got closer, I wished I had a Thompson machine gun instead of my eight-shot rifle.

The sound of the machine guns was constant. Within two hours of the most intensive fighting imaginable, the unthinkable happened. The Germans retreated and we took La Difensa. We scoured the entire top of the mountain for weapon caches and possible booby-traps. We only found dead Germans and our own fallen members.

I walked tall, shouting to the sky and beating my chest. We all knew this was a major victory. I also knew we had a few more mountains to take before we could truly celebrate. When we finished counting our own dead, I realized that our CO was amongst them. He was a Canadian from British Columbia and I respected him almost as much as I respected Colonel Frederick.

"We should put our calling cards on the dead German bodies and give them back for burial." Scotty had an odd sense of humour but we were all nodding our heads.

"Maybe leave the bodies for someone else," Caz said. "I have no intention of touching them—except to leave our cards."

"Agreed," I said. Then, in silence, I pulled the red cards from my pocket and began putting one on each of the dead Germans. Each card had the unit's insignia on it with the words *"Das dicke ende kommt noch!"* I was told that it meant, 'the worst is yet to come'.

MIGIZI

When we had finished, we returned to our own fallen friends and bowed our heads. I could feel warm tears on my face and I would swear that the others were crying as well. But we were all camouflaged by the rain.

CHAPTER NINE

The Devil's Brigade

"I like it," I said.

"I *love* it," Caz said. He was grinning from ear to ear and smoking a cigar. I don't know where he found it.

"It sums us up," Scotty said.

"Do you think it was the Colonel or did someone actually find some dead Kraut's diary?" I was a bit sceptical of the stories. I thought it was more likely a propaganda move by Colonel Frederick.

"Who cares? The media is calling us the Devil's Brigade and the Krauts are afraid of us."

"I love stealing their chickens," I said.

"And their booze," Scotty said.

"I'd steal their women but I haven't seen any yet," Caz said.

"I think it's those cards," I said.

"Probably. They don't know how we can creep in there and do what we do without any noise. I thought they were supposed to be the best soldiers in the world." Caz blew a smoke ring to emphasise this point.

"Whatever we're doing, we need to keep on doing it. We're rattling them. They think we're ten times the size we are. Hell, our regiment is barely three companies now."

"Quiet, my friend," Caz cautioned. "Loose lips sink ships, and all that." He smiled and we all toasted our victories and fallen friends.

Anzio was where we became known as the Devil's Brigade. Perhaps it was the shoe polish we wore when we went on night patrol or the stickers and cards we left on the dead bodies we left behind. We would patrol as far as half a mile behind German lines and leave our stickers on guard posts and supply dumps. It was purely psychological but caused the enemy to fortify its positions and commit more to their lines than they wanted. We were making an impact.

Anzio was a critical battle we needed to win before we could take Rome. We were up against a combined German and Italian troop strength of seventy thousand men. It included the Hermann Göering Division and the 35th Panzergrenadier Regiment of the 16th SS Panzergrenadier Division.

From my perspective, I only needed to know that they were the enemy and that we were the good guys. I watched my guys' backs and they watched mine. Somehow, we survived.

Somehow, we won.

We were always the first in to see action. We scouted the area and provided the Intel for the larger forces behind us. We engaged with the enemy when we made contact. Our specialty was moving and killing at night. We killed with a knife because a gun would alert them to our position. We knew that every piece of Intel was important—possibly the difference between winning and losing battles. I believe that we helped win the battles.

"You notice that we are first into Rome as well," Scotty said.

"I don't mind," I said. "It's a nice walk and the girls are even prettier than in Naples." This time, I allowed myself to be kissed.

"We've done our job. Why not enjoy some perks?" Caz said. He was in heaven.

The previous night, the entire 1st Special Service Force entered Rome and secured the bridges from being destroyed by the fleeing Wehrmacht. We were now, technically, pursuing the retreating Germans.

In reality, we were enjoying the friendly hospitality of the Romans.

"You will need to be careful, Caz," I said. "You're going to pick up something."

"And you won't?" he laughed.

"I'm more discerning," I said. Neither of us could refrain from smiling.

"Both of you are incorrigible," Scotty said. I had begun to understand him long ago, but he still used words I didn't understand.

"You're just jealous," Caz said.

"Of what?"

"Of our good looks. Geezer and I look like men and, well, you look a little funny."

"What's that supposed to mean?"

"I mean, you like to wear dresses. The girls pick up on those things."

Scotty was used to the jibes and ignored Caz. He was married and carried the picture of his wife and new-born child in his pocket. He never cheated and was one of the best fighters in the brigade. He had nothing to prove and was strong enough to know that. He ignored Caz and changed the subject.

"At least we can congratulate suicide boy here. What were you thinking, Geez?"

I shrugged. "I don't know. It seemed like the thing to do at the time."

"Hey, I know we're all a little more crazy than brave, but that thing you did will get you a medal."

"It was nothing," I said. "You both would have done the same."

"Really? Stuck behind enemy lines, within six hundred feet of their artillery assembly area, knowing that you can be killed at any time?"

"We do that every day," I said.

"Sure, with tanks and guns and weapons pointing back. You sauntered into the field and shook your fist at them. That's not sane."

"I needed to reconnect the communications cable. Their stupid antics somehow blew up our line." I was trying to downplay it but I knew it was crazy. At the time, it seemed like the only thing to do.

"Let me go through this again," Scotty said. "You are a mile behind enemy lines. You are close enough to see the enemy putting their weapons together. You dress as a farmer and begin to hoe the ground, walking slowly from your hut to the point where the cable was blown. You make a show of shaking your fist at them and then us. You get to the cable and pretend to tie your shoes. You fix the cable. As a result, we get invaluable Intel that helps turn the battle in our favour. We knocked out four German batteries. How can you not see yourself getting a medal?"

I became shy. "I knew if I didn't connect that cable, you both could get killed. I couldn't live with that."

We carried on walking in silence. I felt Scotty's arm around me, then Caz's. It was all I could do to prevent myself from crying.

*
*

On September 1, 1944, I was sent with Caz and Scotty to scout out German positions near L'Escarène on the French-Italian border. On our way back to report, we heard gunfire being exchanged and decided to see what was happening. Besides, we thought, any action would need to be part of our report.

"There, just behind the group of trees. Germans." Scotty was whispering and getting his rifle ready. I had already got mine ready. Caz was doing the same.

"Who are they firing on?" I asked. I had been made Reconnaissance Sergeant shortly before the Anzio landing so, technically, I was in charge.

"It looks like a motley crew of partisans," Caz said.

"French partisans," I whispered as much to myself as them. "They have to fight them but they're going to get slaughtered. They're outnumbered. I say we engage."

They both agreed.

"The Colonel may have our hides if we don't get our report back to him," I muttered.

"It won't matter," grinned Scotty. "We'll be dead."

"We'd better be. If not, he'll kill us!" I said it in jest but I believed it. "Caz, concentrate on those Krauts on the elevated positions. They're stationary. Should be straightforward shots. Scotty, take those behind the trees. I'll take the ones on the move. Wait for my shot before engaging."

I no longer felt the stones that jutted up from the ground into my belly, nor the brambles that scratched against my clothes. The day was clear with blue skies and little wind. I knew I could hit at a thousand yards. Those Germans were a lot closer than that. I took aim and dropped the man closest to the Frenchmen.

I felt the percussion of the two subsequent shots as I focussed on the next man. I dropped him as well. I didn't look to see whether Scotty or Caz were successful. I had my mission; they had theirs.

The Krauts stopped firing at the partisans and took cover from their unknown assailants. We didn't stop firing until we dropped every one of them. We stayed under cover long enough to know that there were no more heroes and any breathing Germans had fled. We began to close the gap between ourselves and came in contact with the French leader. He saw our uniforms and saluted. We saluted back.

"*Merci beaucoup,* I must thank you and your men for what you have done," he started. "I thought that was our last battle."

"I'm sure you would have done the same for us," I replied. He came close and gave me a firm handshake and then pulled me in and kissed both my cheeks. When he stepped back there were tears in his eyes.

"Where is the rest of your company?" he asked as he brought his emotions under control.

I looked around at Caz and Scotty, then back at the French commander. "Here."

What followed was some swearing in French that I didn't understand. I looked to Caz and he shook his head as if to say *I'll tell you later*.

"Sergeant, that has been the greatest display of sniping I have ever been witness to. I am recommending the *Croix de Guerre* for you and your men. I will send a courier to General de Gaulle as soon as possible."

"Sir, you are too kind. My men and I were passing through and couldn't not help. I wish you well. Good day." I was stunned at the reception and thought the offer of a medal a bit too much, but my report was still due. I continued back to base.

I submitted my report and led my unit back into action immediately. I was tired but the opportunity was now, not some point in the future. In the end, our unit captured an entire German battalion of one thousand men. After that, I slept. I had been awake without food or water for seventy-two hours and walked over forty-five miles across mountainous terrain. I felt I had deserved a good sleep. In exchange, the Americans awarded the American Silver Star to me.

On December 5th, 1944, the 1st Special Service Force was disbanded and I was sent to England with Scotty and Caz. I volunteered to join the British-Canadian detachment on its way to Germany itself. Scotty and Caz went back to Canada. I never saw or heard from Scotty and Caz again.

CHAPTER TEN

The Concentration Camps

My feet hit the pummelled earth to the east of the Rhine River, near Wesel, Germany. The ground was churned up worse than anything I had seen before—and I had seen a lot. I had attached myself to the 6th Airborne Division of the British Army. They were working with the Black Bulls, also known as the British 11th Armoured Division. Before we jumped from the planes at night, 3,500 artillery guns targeted German positions and made safe our landing area. I must have been one of the first hundred guys that jumped. I was missing Caz and Scotty but found some new friends. It was dangerous making new friends as they sometimes didn't make it.

"Looks like something out of a dream or nightmare," I said as I looked at all the floating mushrooms in the night sky. I was gathering up my parachute and talking to no one in particular.

"Yeah, like that radio guy Orson Welles. Got everyone going crazy with that Mars invasion. Imagine what he'd be saying if he saw this!"

The voice came from behind me and I looked around. All I saw was his grinning teeth in the moonlight. "At least the ground is soft," I said.

"Yeah, like hamburger," he said. "Good for landing. Bad for walking."

He had a point. I became concerned about twisting or breaking something in the irregular holes amidst churned earth. "I wonder if any unexploded ordnance is still in the ground."

"I wouldn't worry about it," he said. "By the time you find out, you'll be dead." More grinning. I decided that I liked this guy.

"My name's Migizi. Everyone calls me Geezer."

"Good one," he said. "I'm Tommy. Everyone calls me Tommy."

I laughed and was already walking in the direction of our objective, trying to decide where to ditch my parachute. He came in next to me.

"Been in this war long?" He asked.

"In action since '43. You?"

"This is my first mission. Where you from?"

"Canada."

"That explains the accent. I couldn't figure out what a Yank was doing attached to us."

I liked that all he noticed was the accent. He saw me as a man and it was why I was the first to volunteer to jump and why I stayed on instead of going home like Caz and Scotty.

"I used to be with the 1st Special Service Force. You may have heard of us? The media called us the Devil's Brigade."

"No fawking way," he stopped and put his hand on my arm. "Let me shake your hand. I didn't believe some of the stories. They said you guys moved without making a sound, and killed with your bare hands."

"Don't believe everything you hear but we did our bit." I was bursting with pride but trying not to show it.

"Wait until the other guys hear about this. You won't be buying drinks for the next few nights, Geezer."

"Just keep your eyes open. You don't know when Jerry's going to show himself." I knew we were talking too much, but the sounds of the shelling was constant in the background. I sometimes wondered how we weren't hit when jumping from the plane.

"Yes, Sergeant," he said as he glanced at my rank.

We walked in silence and I could feel our numbers increase on the ground as we made our way to our first objective. Sixteen thousand paratroopers were landing with me. I didn't feel alone for long.

"We need to secure Schnappenberg first. I want to move on to our primary objective of securing the three bridges that cross the River Issel ASAP. If we don't do that, we can't get our tanks into Germany as quickly as we'd like."

Tommy nodded and we could see each platoon forming around their COs. There was no reason to not talk as the sound of the planes overhead was continuous.

I fought every battle as though it was my last— with every ounce of energy I could muster. Tommy survived alongside me and we did our part in securing the villages of Schnappenberg and Hamminkeln and the three bridges over the River Issel. All this meant was that we were now joining the Black Bulls in their advance into the heart of northern Germany. Their objective was Hamburg and the surrounding area known as Schleswig-Holstein. I didn't worry about the names and made sure I kept as dry as possible and slept as much as possible. Food was terrible compared to my time with the Devil's Brigade. I never understood why we were disbanded.

"It feels like the end, doesn't it?" Tommy said. He was much younger than me, probably no more than eighteen. He was like a puppy that had attached himself to me.

"It's not over until it's over," I said. "I was a sniper and we can do a lot of damage if we get in position. Always watch yourself. Stay close to me and do what I do."

"Yes, Sergeant. You bet."

I couldn't reprimand him for his enthusiasm. We were a mass of soldiers and I couldn't understand how they kept any sense of order in the chaos. I was used by my superiors and I utilized the talent under me. It was organised chaos. All I knew was that I was still walking in the mud while the officers rode in jeeps.

Each day began to blur as it became clear that this was a mopping up exercise. We lost two thousand men crossing the Rhine and many more casualties. After that, I think Jerry's will was broken.

"Tommy, do you realize that not one foreign boot set foot on German soil during World War I?"

"That a fact?"

"That's what I'm told," I said. "Now, we are marching to Hamburg and Berlin. This war should be over in a month."

"That'll be fine with me," he said. "I'll ask Tina to marry me and we'll settle somewhere I can find a job. How about you, Geez?"

I paused. I had never thought past the moment. It was a dangerous thing to do and I knew it was important to live today if tomorrow was going to be possible. If I didn't make it past today, tomorrow would never happen. It kept me alive by keeping me focussed.

"Ask me when it happens," I finally said. No way was I going to jinx this now.

"Do you have any idea why we haven't moved in days while everyone else has disappeared north?"

"You haven't been in the army long enough, Tommy. Enjoy any time you have to sleep and relax. There's plenty of time to fight in the future."

"I hear they've found something nasty. Something about a camp?"

"I don't know anything more than you do," I said. "We'll deal with whatever we are told to do. I'm a Canadian, you're a Brit, and we're both being led by the Yanks. It's their show. I have a feeling if there is a babysitting job, they'll be giving it to us."

"I guess it's better than getting our brains splattered everywhere by a sniper," he said.

"That's the spirit. Gotta smoke?"

✳

On April 12th, 1945, we were instructed to take charge of a German detention camp. Our commanders had negotiated a deal with the SS commanders to allow the Black Bulls to occupy the camp and continue towards Hamburg. I was told I would be babysitting at this camp.

"I guess it'll be more of the same," I said. "Women hugging and kissing us, thankful to be alive and liberated. Men crying at the shame they had to live through."

"You must have seen so much," Tommy said.

"I've seen a fair deal. I'm still struck at how they treated us in Rome. Their family members were dead, some buried in the rubble beneath our feet, and they gave us their last morsels of food and wine. The women gave us their bodies and it felt as though they were waking from a nightmare to realize it had happened. They needed someone to hold and make them feel safe."

"I guess you did what you had to do," Tommy said with his ever-present smirk.

"I couldn't take their food." I didn't say any more on the subject to Tommy.

We were marching towards a place called Bergen-Belsen.

"I hope you had your shots," I said.

"Why?"

"The place we're going to is full of sick people."

"How'd you know?"

"I've overheard a few conversations. There are some reports of scenes out of nightmares, but I can't imagine anything worse than the battles we've been through." I could see the trucks where doctors and other medical staff had been taken ahead of us to prepare the site.

"Doesn't look so bad," Tommy said.

I had to agree. The site looked like any other German camp. Lots of barracks with a fence around it. I could make out the gun towers and was able to see the barbed wire along the top of the fencing. "They sure knew how to make a decent fence," I said.

"Huh?"

"Nothing. Let's see what they need us for."

"Inside," came the voice of one of the officers. His face was hard and his eyes red.

"Yes, sir," I said. "Any specific instructions?"

"Find a place to bury the dead."

"Excuse me, sir?"

"Go inside, Sergeant. This one isn't in the manuals."

I offered him a cigarette and he took it. I lit his, then Tommy's, then mine. We went through the entrance gate and saw people in stripes, presumably prisoners, walking in a daze. It took a while for me to understand what was wrong with the picture.

"They're very frail," Tommy said.

"Yeah."

"Holy crap, Geezer, look over there."

We walked briskly so as not to make too much contact with the prisoners. When I saw what he was pointing to, I stopped walking. Then I changed direction and walked directly towards it.

"There must be thousands," I said. I pulled out another cigarette without thinking and gave one to Tommy. We used our existing cigarette to light the new one.

"They don't have any flesh," he whispered.

In front of us was a pile of bodies that stretched as far as we could see, stacked five high.

"They must have been dead for weeks, maybe months. These bastards didn't bury them?"

"I guess they felt the winter would keep them. The snow is gone and they are beginning to rot."

"Stay clear," I said. "They'll be full of disease."

"You don't need to tell me that twice, Geez."

"Let's see what else this place has in store for us." I kept those skeletal piles in my periphery as I took in the barracks. They were wooden and set on blocks. Nothing particularly interesting about them. I noticed that a lot of prisoners were beginning to move around.

"Shall we look inside?" Tommy asked.

We approached a quiet barrack where I only noticed a couple of prisoners walking outside. They were smoking and grinning at me. I gave them each a cigarette but kept on walking. I wanted to see what I was going to be babysitting.

There were no lights inside the barracks and the doorway was the only source of light. It took a while for my eyes to adjust to the darkness. Inside, I began to make out the shapes of bodies on the beds. There were beds all the way to the ceiling with barely enough room for the person to turn, and definitely not able to sit up. They were set out in rows for the length of the barracks. All I could see were eyes that turned to look at me, their bodies too tired to move.

"Geez, the smell is worse than a barn," Tommy said.

I turned and left. Tommy followed.

MIGIZI

We walked in silence as we came across the women's barracks. They barely wore clothes and didn't seem to care. Many wore the uniforms but, inside, the weaker ones cowered in their bunks. One woman handed me a bundle that I opened. I recoiled at the sight of her baby inside; he must have died weeks before. Its skin had gone black.

I saw skeletons with green skin as they decomposed. I had seen dead people before; I had killed many myself. But the desiccated black skin pulled tightly over the skeletons was hard to bear. It wasn't just one skeleton. Not a hundred. Not even a thousand. It was tens of thousands of skeletons. Thirteen thousand skeletons were dead and lay decomposing on the ground. Sixty thousand walking skeletons filled the barracks and the spaces. I couldn't understand how they were alive.

"Tommy, this is the lowest point of the war for me. I didn't think it possible for me to be shocked."

"And the disease, Geezer, we need to deal with that sooner or later."

"The docs will tell us what to do. I'm no good with this stuff. Point me at a target and tell me to shoot it and I'll do it. Point me at a man and tell me to kill him, fine. Ask me to babysit the living dead, and I'm lost."

"Smoke?"

"I've never wanted one more in my life," I said. We had toured the complex and it took longer than I had anticipated. I knew we would be digging mass graves when I saw the military bulldozers arriving. I began to fear we would be digging the graves ourselves.

A group of fifteen men drifted towards us listlessly, their bodies covered with their prisoners' stripes that hung without form. Their faces were gaunt and their eyes bulged. They said nothing. They looked at us and took a step closer. They either couldn't talk or didn't have the energy. I watched them, transfixed, wondering how any human could live like this.

There were no cheers or tears, just silence as we assessed the situation. I knew we would be put to work dealing with the dead and the disease. We needed to delouse them and burn the buildings. We needed to find ways to feed them.

My mind was turning over the tasks ahead when I heard a sound that cut through me more deeply than a bullet. It transported me to my childhood and the moment I saw Geezis walk off that window ledge. It put me on my cot, not unlike the ones in the barracks, in school all those years ago. I felt the rough clothing of the Father, his smells brought close to me. I could feel the sting of the strap again as if I had just been struck. I felt a fear I had never felt since I put on my uniform.

It was the sound of a baby crying.

CHAPTER ELEVEN

Operation Magic Carpet

"Doesn't feel like magic to me," a voice said.

I didn't respond.

"I can't wait to get home," the same voice said. "Hold my Mary next to me, dance until our feet are sore, and, well, you know, have a family."

I don't know why some people needed to talk. I was lying on my cot, minding my own business. I didn't know if I wanted to go home. I didn't know what home was until I joined the army. And I sure as hell wasn't talking to this joker next to me.

"You don't talk much, do you?" He sat up and looked around, trying to find someone else to talk to. Everyone was either sleeping or ignoring him more effectively than me. "My name's Hobbs."

"Migizi. Everyone calls me Geezer."

"Hi Geezer. Great name. Bet you can't believe you survived, eh? I'll tell you a thing or two. Thought I'd

177

never make it out alive. My best friend and most of my company were killed on the landings. You know, D-Day?"

I was beginning to dislike this guy. No one I knew ever talked about those landings. It was a slaughter, a rational suicide made for the greater good. It made no sense who made it and who didn't. The water and sand bled with the brave and cowardly alike. I didn't reply.

"You see any action?"

"A little," I said.

"I saw enough to last a lifetime. It's the reason I can't sleep. If I close my eyes, I see them. The bloated bodies, never buried. The sound of broken men crying. That was the worst. It's bad enough to be shot at, bombed, and stabbed. But the crying's the worst."

I thought about that baby in the concentration camp. "Yeah," I said.

He pulled out a flask and offered me a swig. I shook my head. He took a long drink.

"I think about my daddy and what he went through in the first war. They say they lost a million men and didn't gain one mile." He was looking into the distance and I could recognize the effects of alcohol taking hold of him. I knew it would end with him crying or fighting. You never knew until it happened. Then it was too late.

"My father was also in the First World War," I said. "He doesn't talk about it. He said that the horrors of war had no place in a home. I never understood what he meant until now."

"To your father." Hobbs lifted his flask and took a drink. I could see a tear on his cheek.

I nodded in appreciation to his toast and got up to walk outside. The room was full of hundreds of service men sleeping, some smelling like a brewery, and others snoring. I couldn't sleep and I didn't want to talk to Hobbs or anyone for that matter.

Outside, the ocean air was cold. I had remained at the Bergen-Belsen camp for a couple of months as the bodies needed to be buried and the sick attended to. The COs decided to burn every building to the ground to combat the disease that was rife. I could still see the green and black skin of the dead when I closed my eyes. But the living dead scared me more. They had lost their souls and their bodies walked the earth waiting to die. I didn't know what kept them alive.

I learned a lot about what happened when I was stationed there. The guards took all of the prisoners' belongings when they arrived. Each prisoner was given a uniform to wear. Each prisoner was given a new identity. They no longer were known by the names their parents gave them. They were known by the number tattooed onto their forearm. Their days consisted of working hard—from making shoes to shells. They never left, never saw their families again. The government policy was to crush the soul from them and then kill their bodies when they could no longer provide any use to the Reich. It was institutional genocide.

Those who survived had a vacant look in their eyes. They wanted to live but no longer had the energy to care. They were in the hands of fate, or God, or whomever was in charge of the camp at the time. We tried to feed them but their bodies rejected food. It took a while before we came up with a solution that their bodies would accept. Meanwhile, they continued to die.

"Whatcha thinking about?" Hobbs' voice started up again next to me. I could smell him despite the wind.

"Nothing much," I lied.

"They're calling this Operation Magic Carpet, you know that?"

"I didn't." I didn't care.

"They're going to whisk us all back home and tuck us into bed and pretend it all didn't happen."

It was the first thing he said that made sense and I turned to look at him. "Like a bad dream," I said.

"Can I tell you something, Geezer?"

I shrugged.

"I lied about Mary. There won't be anyone waiting for me when I get home. I haven't received a letter from her for over a year. I'm no fool. I know what happens. She got tired of waiting for me." The tears on his face gleamed in the moonlight. He didn't bother to wipe them away.

"I'm sorry."

"I know. Not much you can do about it. I can't sleep. I'm getting antsy thinking about returning. I want to stay in the army but they don't have any need for me anymore. They're demobilizing."

"That's a good thing, isn't it?" I said.

"What, not needing me?"

"Demobilizing. War's over."

"There's always another war. I just wish it came sooner than later. Then I won't have to tell lies to those dumb-asses in my hometown. How can they know what we've been through? No one chooses to see your best friend's head explode like a pumpkin next to you, his brains and bloody bits all over you.

Or those body parts as you go through the enemy lines, blown apart by artillery."

I could see Hobbs working himself up. He took another long drink and began to cry. His whole body convulsed. I put my arms around him, trying to comfort his pain. It was the same pain I carried, but I had been doing so for much longer.

We were all alone on the deck. The moon was bright like a faint light and the ship made its way ever onwards. I wanted to get him to go back to sleep or, at least, away from the railing.

"Hobbs, do you have anything to eat? I'm starving."

"Sorry, Geezer. I only have my drink." He must have been going at it for a while because he was beginning to sway.

"Hold on and I'll find a sandwich. I always keep a spare in times of an emergency," I said. It was true. It was a habit that kept my body strong. "A good sandwich is as handy as a grenade," I added. I wanted to see him smile.

He did and waved to me. I took it as him being OK and I disappeared into the room below and found my cot. I dug the sandwich out of my rucksack and returned to the deck. I saw Hobbs sitting on the railing.

"Hobbs! I got your sandwich."

He turned and smiled at me. "Thanks, Geezer. You're one of the good guys." And with that, he lifted himself off the rail so that he was standing on the lowest rail but on the outside. He somehow stood at attention, saluted the night sky and let himself fall.

"Hobbs!" I screamed, running towards the rail. I saw nothing, not even a splash. Blackness everywhere.

I felt my body shake from the shock but also from the memory of my best friend, Geezis. It was as though I was not allowed to keep my pain inside any longer. I could no longer feel physical pain from those ghosts but the images that came flooding over me caused me to sweat and shake as I gripped the railing. My hair blew flat against my scalp as the ship continued on relentlessly. I knew I would have to report Hobbs' death. But, first, I slipped to the deck and began to weep.

Out of my tears wept the blood that flowed from cuts and bruises all those years ago. The strap, the fists, the other things. I saw the red-faced nun beating me and the way Brother Thomas took Geezis out of the room. I remember Father O'Flaherty holding me close as I cried that night. I remembered what he did to me that night, the first of many. My shame as I returned bloodied the first time and the pride as I was excused by O'Flaherty from working for a week on account of my hurt.

The following years never got better.

I felt the night air against my skin and the rails against my back. The cold of the deck slowly began to creep through my trousers. I could feel the layers of paint against the immovable steel. And it made me think of how much steel was blown apart these last few years. Nothing was stable. I needed to report Hobbs' death. I needed to cry. I needed to mourn those years of hurt; that pain that never went away.

I got off more easily than some of the others. O'Flaherty didn't allow them to beat me after that night. I became his pet. He disciplined me his own way. I probably deserved it. It made me who I am today. But I never breathed a word to anyone. If Geezis was around, I could talk to him. I know now that he was someone's pet before me.

"Pull yourself together, Geezer," I said out loud.

"Now, stand up." I did.

"Find the CO and report Hobbs' death. On the double."

I pushed the tears back into my eyes and closed myself to the past. It was how I had stayed alive and how I would continue to stay alive.

CHAPTER
TWELVE

Finding Family

When we all returned, there was a parade and I attended, all polished and looking proud in my medals. I was noticed and politicians began to invite me to talk about my experiences. I was heralded as the 'most decorated Indian' in Canadian history. All I heard from that 'compliment' was that I was an Indian. They forgot I was a man. At no time did they refer to me as a Canadian. I tried to live in their world, but it always felt like I was a temporary visitor who was tolerated. I had no purpose other than to allow them to congratulate themselves at how well their Indian policy was working. I decided to go home.

"Migizi!"

"Mom!" I hadn't seen her in over sixteen years. I almost didn't recognize her.

"Son, you look so strong. Your father would have been proud."

I stopped. "Dad?"

"I didn't want to upset you. You were in the newspapers and all the big shots wanted to have their picture with you. You deserved the praise."

"When?"

"Last month." Her happiness drained at the memory.

"How could you?" My body became heavy and I needed to sit down. I could feel myself slipping away. My dad couldn't die. Soldiers died. I could die; not him. My breathing became laboured as I tried to digest what she was saying.

"There was nothing we could do. He began having pains in his chest. We called the ambulance but it took six hours before they arrived." She sat on the ground next to me. The rest of the tribe must have known as they didn't come out to see me. I could see the curtains twitching as I felt my mother lean against me and begin to cry.

"I'm sorry I wasn't here."

"You made him proud. You should have seen the way his eyes looked when he talked about you." She wiped away her tears with her reddened hands. The tears disappeared in the creases on her face. She forced herself to smile and tried to get up. I helped her. "Come inside. You have people waiting for you."

She grabbed my arm, partly for support and partly to guide me. I had no idea which house we were going to.

"We don't need to do this now," I said. "I'm not leaving."

"You need to see your sons and your daughter."

My body went numb as it underwent one shock after another. I knew I needed to face Theresa again. I looked forward to seeing Winona and holding her in my arms. She hadn't been born when I left. Asin and Makwa were probably big boys by now.

I opened the front door to see myself with a baby in my arms.

"Asin? Is that you?" I put down my bags and began walking towards him. He looked at me like a stranger.

"Father?"

"You look the image of me. Whose baby is that?"

"That's your grandson," Theresa emerged from behind our two boys.

At first, I was unable to respond. Asin raised the baby and handed him to me. "What's his name?"

"Ishkode," Asin said. "I met his mother during a party that ended with the house burning down. I thought it was a good name."

"It means 'fire'. What a lovely name," I said. I was holding him as carefully as I could. My bones ached from the abuse of army life. I touched his raven-black hair and smiled at a thought I couldn't put my finger on.

"Are you staying?" Theresa motioned towards the kitchen table with food on it.

"If I can." I didn't know what to expect. I was looking for her other three children.

"If you're looking for Waabizii, Niimi and Myeegun, they're out with their father." She must have noticed my searching eyes and decided to put me out of my misery.

"Look," I said. "I'm as much a stranger as a father. I've been gone longer than they've been alive. I don't expect to be wanted. I understand if you want me to leave." I felt less stress under German artillery fire than I was feeling at this moment. Guilt and shame were overwhelming.

I felt an arm link mine. "Don't talk nonsense. You're the father of our children. We're family." Theresa had put on some weight and looked happy. I could feel her strength as she guided me to the table. "Can I get you a drink?"

"No, thanks. Not for me." I hadn't had a drink since the raven visited me.

She looked up, surprised. "I'm proud of you, Migizi."

I felt the hand of my mother on my head briefly as she passed me and began helping Theresa with the food. Asin must have nodded to someone hidden in the corner and a girl came forward and took her child. I found out later that her name was Aki. Asin sat next to me and Aki tended to baby Ishkode. Makwa, my other son, sat on the other side of me.

When a beautiful girl, almost a woman, sat down, I looked at the others to see who she might be. I needn't have bothered. When I looked at her carefully, I could see her mother in her and my unfortunate nose that she inherited. She had long, blue-black hair that reached down her back.

"Winona?" I sat forward to get a better look.

"*Imbaabaa,*" she said. My father.

"*Nindaanis,*" I said. My daughter.

She reached out and I held her hand on the kitchen table as Theresa and Mother set out the food. My two sons sat stoically next to me. I had come home.

*

I didn't realize that I earned money while fighting in the army. As a result, I had enough to buy a home in Winnipeg. When I told the acting Chief, he gave me a house on the reserve instead. My money was no good on the reserve because there was nothing to buy. None of us owned anything.

"By law, you can't own your home," Chief Maengun said.

"I've been away from the system so long, I had forgotten. I'd be honoured to live here," I said.

"We can't own land or farm or practice our culture," the Chief continued. "Soon, we'll be no more."

"Maybe I can help?"

"We must all try in ways that we can to help. We must be able to speak our language and practice our religion. It is a right guaranteed to everyone else but us. Didn't you fight for those freedoms?" He looked at me through the smoke and I thought I could see a slight smile.

"I fought because my father fought."

"You are an honourable man, Migizi. But look around you. What has changed? You have fought a war for a country that still requires us to go to the RCMP and get a piece of paper signed allowing us to leave the reserve. This pass system is illogical and contrary to what they say they want—our assimilation to their ways. We all live on a piece of land not much bigger than a large farm that a

Canadian can own outright. We need to get permission to leave this parcel of land and we can't build on it or farm it or sell it. The Canadian government takes care of us by starving us, taking our children and killing our culture. In return, all I hear from them is that we are drunk, wild Indians with no soul and no God. They think they are doing the right thing. I ask you: do you feel like a Canadian? Or an equal?"

I came to talk about the house he was giving me. I wasn't expecting to try and solve the problems of our people. "I haven't thought about it," I said honestly.

"If you don't, who will? Your children? Their children? You have seen the world. You have travelled to places that are just names on a map or words in a conversation to others."

"What do you want me to do? Kill all the politicians?" I expected the Chief to laugh with me, but his face was deadpan.

"That won't help. The pass system was put in place to control our rebellion as the railway cut through our lands. They will use our violence to further justify their outrages. Instead, they wait for us to die of strangulation."

"We can leave and live in the cities, like I did."

"Migizi, you are strong and you are only one person. Many of us will get lost with no roots in the concrete and brick of cities. There is no soul in cities. We are people of the land and we can only live with the land, in harmony."

I thought about how I was saved by the Sagkeeng Nation near Pine Falls and wished I hadn't said anything about the cities. Winnipeg nearly destroyed me as well. I nodded and remained silent. The Chief and the other elders sat with me in the sweat lodge and we pondered on what was said.

✳

I was shy at first, at least until she moved in. Nagam was the first woman I loved since Kim. Theresa was the mother of my children and would always hold a place in my heart, but there was so much pain when I saw her. Nagam was a few years younger than me and she became pregnant shortly after moving in.

"You know that Ishkode is off to school this year?" Nagam was beginning to show and liked to walk naked in our house. I liked it when she did that. I was never comfortable enough with my body to be naked all the time.

"The same one I went to?" I couldn't believe my grandson was old enough for school. And I didn't want him to go through the hell I went through.

"And me," she said. She was warm as she sat on my lap. When she kissed me gently, nothing could hurt me. The memories of Father O'Flaherty began to fade.

"I wish we could send him to a proper school. One that didn't beat his soul out of him."

She looked at me like she was going to say something but decided against it. "It's the law. If we don't send him, they'll pick him up and take him."

"I don't have to like it," I said. I gave her a kiss and a light tap on her behind. I wanted to visit with my grandson before he went into that place.

They lived only a few doors down. I was proud of Asin and Makwa as they grew into fine men. They had more children and they stayed off the alcohol. I saw them working with the Chief to build more homes and make the reserve a better place. It was tough, as money was always tight. I helped hunt and fish to provide food, but there was little else I could do.

"So Ishkode is a big boy today," I said as I lifted him into my arms. He squirmed and I let him go, but not after I gave him a kiss.

"I wish I could run away into the bush with him," Asin said. His face was set and I could see turmoil behind his eyes.

"I wish so too, son." I put my hand on his shoulder. I could see his wife inside; she looked like she had been crying. I didn't go into their home as they lived with Theresa and I still didn't like being around her new man.

"Dad?"

"Yes, son?"

"Will it get better? I mean, you did all those things and they still treat you like an Indian. You're living here instead of Winnipeg. Was it worth it, going to war?"

I didn't expect that today. "Things must change. And they have gotten a little better since I was a boy. But things take time. All we can do is trust the government to do the right thing. They've recently banned the pass system. That's a start."

Asin looked angry. "Does any Canadian need a pass when they leave their home or town to go shopping or hunting?"

I didn't have a reply to that. It was something I couldn't do anything about. It would change when the government decided it would change.

"Are Canadians arrested if their children don't go to school?"

"I think their children are also rounded up and taken back to school. Truancy isn't tolerated anywhere."

"But I bet they don't get beaten like we did or are told they couldn't speak their language."

I had no response to that. Instead, I tried to be hopeful. "Asin, things will get better. I don't know how or when, but they will. How is your mother?"

"She's worse than Aki. They're both crying. It makes me so angry." He hit his fist against the door. "I can't do anything to protect my son."

"Have you prayed? Spend some time in the sweat lodge. It helped me a lot. Maybe, it'll help your anger as well."

"Dad, you …" His voice trailed off as he shook himself. "OK. I'll try." I knew he didn't agree with me but he was a good boy and respected his elders. I loved him more because of it.

When the bus came to pick up Ishkode, we all stood silently watching him get into the bus and disappear into the distance. I never wanted a drink more badly than right then.

Ishkode survived his first year and then his second year at school. He had almost forgotten who we were when he finally returned after year one. By year two, he no longer had the same light in his eyes. I assumed he was growing up.

My other son, Makwa, watched as his girl Megis left for school as Ishkode was entering year three. We all watched as the older boy held her hand and entered the bus. Again, our faces felt warm tears as they disappeared into the distance.

*
*

It was 1956 and my firstborn son with Nagam was three years old. I had had enough of living on the reserve, not working, and listening to the same conversations over and over again. I loved hunting and the community that existed, but I needed more. I told Nagam that we were going to live in Winnipeg. She smiled and told me she was pregnant again. I couldn't be happier. I bought a small house on Sherbrook, off Portage. It would be the perfect home for us to raise our new family. We were also close to good schools and hospitals. I could walk Myeengun to school every day when the time came and then go to work. My head was full of an idyllic future.

"Hello? Yes. One moment please. I'll get him." Nagam put the phone down and called me. I had heard it ring but still loved hearing her voice call my name. I loved that it was our phone and our home.

"Yes, this is Migizi." I felt like a Canadian when I answered the phone like that. I could have been one of those fathers in the movies with his starched clothing and perfect family. I couldn't have been happier.

"Uh huh. Yeah. Are you sure?" Nagam came closer to me as she heard my voice change. I could feel her arm going around my waist. "No. No, *please God,* no!" I had to sit down. The phone was in the kitchen so I pulled up a chair and slumped down. "When did it happen?" My body was becoming limp. "What! And we're only finding out now?" I was standing and Nagam became frightened. The baby in the other room began crying. "No funeral? Just like that? Have you called the RCMP? Yeah, I know. Probably wouldn't help. We'll be there as soon as we can. OK. Goodbye." I put the phone back on the receiver and sat down again. I put my hands over my face.

I felt her hands in my hair and smelled the faint scent of her perfume as she stood next to me. She didn't say a thing. She stood next to me and put my head against her and let me cry.

"He's dead," I finally said. "Ishkode's dead."

"What happened?" Her hands were stroking my hair and neck and I held on to her like a child.

"He got sick and died. They buried him and only told Asin today. He died a month ago. They buried him like a dog outside of the school grounds." I could visualize the burials I had witnessed. I saw the infirmary room with all the sick children, then they were all gone. But the room always filled. Bodies would disappear. Many were buried, but only a handful as Christians. "Nine years old. What did they do to him?"

Nagam nodded but didn't say anything. Other than the Chief, no one spoke about what happened at the schools. Asin's anger when Ishkode left was a rare exception. I felt strangely outside of their silence. I wanted to scream or kill something. I wanted to drink.

"I'll get you whiskey if you need it," she said. She saw the look in my eyes, the way I held my body. I was her warrior and I looked defeated.

"No. Please don't bring whiskey into this house," I said. "Only because I want it more than I can ever remember. And because I don't want our son to have a drunk Indian father."

I could see tears form and then fall down Nagam's cheeks. She came next to me and held me tight. "Bravery is being afraid and still facing it," she said. "You are the bravest man I know."

Her words gave me the strength to stand up. I went to my son and picked him up. "Let's go for a walk, Myeengun. Let's go and see something normal; something that isn't a disaster involving drugs or alcohol or death."

*
*

It was a year later when I received another call. Makwa's daughter, Megis, had died at school. Theresa was able to get there in time and she was buried by our people. I found myself travelling to the reserve again for the worst of all possible reasons.

"I even made myself a doll of sorrow from the hair of Megis," Theresa said. She was cried-out by the time I arrived.

"And how is Makwa's wife taking this?" I asked.

"How do you think? She's mad. She's heartbroken. She wants to burn down the school and kill every sister and brother in it."

She may need to stand in line, I thought. "We need to be strong for her. This is a great sadness." My knees were weak just talking about it. The only reason I was able to keep myself together was the distance between myself and my grandson. I could only imagine what Makwa and his wife and Theresa were going through. They all lived together.

I watched the ceremony in silence, along with the rest of the community. A child should never be buried, and a father should never bury his own child. I was watching my son bury his daughter and it was almost too much to bear. Children are not supposed to witness burials so my son stayed with my wife at the Chief's house. Our house had been given to the next family when we left for Winnipeg.

The ceremonies and prayers lasted four days. Many of the men and women drank alcohol to numb the pain. I refused, so I ended up playing with my son and spending time with Nagam and Theresa. Asin, Makwa, and Winona had all joined those who drank. I didn't blame them.

The next day, we found Theresa, dead, next to where Makwa's little girl was buried. She was just lying there and I thought she was sleeping when we first came across her. She must have taken something and overdosed in her grief. I had no more tears to cry.

Two weeks later, we returned to Winnipeg, glad to be away from the stress and chaos of the reserve.

"There is so much drama," I said to Nagam. "Why can't we have boring lives like Canadians? They worry about which university their child goes to or whether they will be a doctor or lawyer. We worry about whether our children will survive school and, if they do, whether they will kill themselves from the injustices we endure."

My wife was calm and put her hand on me. It had the desired effect and the strain washed away.

"We are building a life on Sherbrook in our own home. You are a wonderful father and husband. We have a beautiful, healthy boy and a wonderful baby girl. You have everything the Canadians have. We have everything I ever dreamed of. Be happy, despite the pain in the world."

I didn't know where she got her wisdom or strength. "You are my world," I said and held her hand. "The reserve is over there and we are over here. They can't touch us. You're right. We can be the masters of our own lives."

I shook off the blackness and settled into the day that was ahead of us. I cut the grass and trimmed the hedges. I tried to pull the weeds but I hated that part. I would leave it for Nagam to do. The yard looked good enough for me. As I sat on my porch drinking a glass of cold tap water, I noticed two uniformed officers at the little fence that surrounded my property. I got up to see what they wanted.

"Can I help you, officers?"

"Yes. Are you Mr. David Bass, also known as Migizi Baswenaazhi?"

"Yes," I said hesitantly.

"And your wife is Esther Stone, also known as Nagam Aan'Aawenh?"

"Yes." My hands began to sweat and my mouth developed the same copper taste I felt before going into battle.

"Can we come in and talk to you?"

I looked at their uniforms and didn't recognize what they were. They didn't look like RCMP or city cops. But they knew who I was and I assume they had a reason to talk to us. "OK." I opened the chain-link gate.

They walked in and waited for me to open the door to the house. We sat around the kitchen table and Nagam came to join us.

"We understand that your grandchildren died and that your first wife committed suicide," the woman told me. They had been given tea and there was very little small talk before she said this.

"Yes," I said eventually. I was stunned at the insensitivity of the question. "I'm still not sure why you are here."

"It has come to our attention that your children may be at risk."

"That's nonsense," Nagam said. Her face was flush and her nostrils were flared. I was half-expecting her to hit them.

"I'm just telling you what we have in our report, ma'am." Only the woman spoke. The male officer just watched and drank his tea.

"I'm a war vet," I said. "I've received the Silver Star and the *Croix de Guerre* as well as the Military Medal. I'm a good father and Nagam is a good mother. I don't know who could have told you such things."

"Sir, I'm only going by what is in the report."

"OK. What does this mean?" I said. I was also getting angry. I was also becoming anxious.

"It means we will need to take them into custody until the complaint has been resolved."

As they said the words, I could feel my body turn cold. I wanted to strangle them. I knew I could kill them with my bare hands. I saw the same reaction in Nagam. Instead of doing anything, we both sat there looking at them.

"We will be around later today to collect them."

I wanted to gouge their eyes out and stab my spoon into their ear. "Will we be able to visit them?" I asked. I began to loathe my own cowardice.

"Not initially. We'll see how the investigation goes. We'll do everything we can to help you clear this up."

The woman in the uniform stood up to leave. The other uniformed officer remained. I guess they figured we'd grab the children and run. They guessed right.

"I'll be back as soon as possible. Thank you for making this an easy transition." She left and I watched her disappear around the corner.

I couldn't talk to my wife. I went to the other room and held my children. Myeengun looked up at me and I saw him through blurry eyes. Shania was playing with the cloth doll my mother made her. She had no idea what was happening.

All I could think about was how I couldn't protect my children.

＊

I watched in numbed horror as they bundled up Myeengun and Shania. I imagined them assigning new names to them and forcing them to speak only English. Nagam no longer held my hand or whispered calming thoughts into my ear. She sat frozen as they took her babies away.

"This is what Chief Maengun told me when I returned back from Europe fifteen years ago. We have no say in our future or our children's future. Nothing changes."

Nagam wasn't listening. She didn't care what the Chief said.

"I am going to see our MP today and try to figure out how to fix this," I said. I wanted to remain positive. Nagam wasn't listening or having any hope in anything I came up with.

"They're gone," she said. It was a quiet resignation. "Like us being taken to those schools or your grandchildren dying in those same schools. What are we, Geez?"

I reached for her to hold her hand. It was unresponsive, as though I was holding a rag doll. "We are who we are," I said. "We're strong. We'll get through this. They do what they do and we survive."

"I'm tired of merely surviving," she said. Her eyes were closed and her back curved as if she could barely hold herself up. "I'm tired of being positive in the face of impossible rules made by faceless people. I'm tired of being an embarrassment for others to manage."

I knew her words spoke the truth. I lived my life as an island, immune to their comments or jokes. I refused to cry because of them. I would make them cry first. My tears were reserved for my family alone.

"We're never going to see our children again, are we?" She shook but the tears never came.

"You can't think like that. We have rights."

"We have no rights. You, of all people, should know that. It's almost 1960 and we still can't vote. Canadians don't think of us as Canadians. And we don't think of ourselves as Canadians. Yet we fight their wars, speak their language, and try to live their culture. We are not them. When are you going to understand this?" Her neck veins stood out and I could see the blotchy colour of her blood rising. I knew enough to agree with her. I didn't want to fight.

"What you say is true, Nagam. But what are we supposed to do?" I wanted her to calm down. I couldn't remember ever seeing her this upset.

"Maybe there is nothing we can do." Her voice lacked any more fight.

"We can talk to the police and the politicians."

"Haven't you been listening? Haven't you learned from your life until now? The police don't listen. The politicians don't help us. We are on our own. And none of us want to fight them."

"Fight? How?"

"Any way possible."

"We can't vote. We can't even be a politician," I said. I didn't want to rub salt into her already open wounds.

"We need to vote. We need to become politicians. We need to change the system from the inside. I hoped for our children to be lawyers or doctors, not some project for some white family who will dress them up for Christmas and Easter and say prayers. Or for them to grow up thinking they are white until they try to date a white girl or boy. Then they'll find out they are just dirty Indians. Who'll be able to help them then?"

I thought back to Kim and felt a cold chill run through me. It was over thirty years ago, a lifetime, yet it marked the beginning of my realization that I didn't belong. I could work hard, dress well, and do what they wanted. But I would always be an Indian. I didn't share my thoughts with Nagam. She was in a dark enough place already.

"I need to sleep," she said. "Can you leave me alone for while? I'm sorry to ask you, but I need time." Her hair that looked so alive as it caught the light now looked dull. Her eyes that bewitched me and calmed my rage looked dim. She could barely meet my eyes as she asked the question. It broke my heart to see her in such pain.

"I'll go for a walk." I stood up to go.

"Migizi?"

I turned, heart wrenching at the sight of my love in such pain. "Yes?"

"I love you."

I leaned over and kissed her gently. "I love you more."

She smiled wearily and nodded. I left.

I walked down Sherbrook towards the Assiniboine River. The street was green with the leaves of trees, each modest house set back from the sidewalk that ran alongside the road. I loved my home and this street. I loved that I could walk to a hospital and that my wife and family would be safe with the Canadian medicine. I had come to appreciate our own medicine but each had its own place. I loved that I could walk along Wellington Crescent towards the parks or just along the river. I preferred the river.

There were a lot of crows in Winnipeg but I was convinced that my raven watched over me. As I walked, I could hear the deep *'kraa'* of the raven alongside the crows' caws, rattles, and clicks. There were the other usual suspects, but the raven was my reminder all those years ago. It saved me. He saved me.

The summer water levels were lower than normal. I liked walking amidst the birch and elm saplings, soon to be mighty trees. I felt life under my feet as I made my way over the decomposed earth. Life lives, then dies. It grows, learns, and then decays. Each tree creates more trees. Each bird creates more birds. And, like nature, we create our own life.

I didn't notice the tiny scratches I got from the slapping of the small branches against my arms and face. My mind was reeling from my children being taken from me. I wanted to scream or shoot someone, but the image that came to my mind was of me shooting myself. I never saw myself killing those I thought I blamed. Deep down, I blamed myself.

By now, I had walked alongside the winding Assiniboine until I had reached the Legislative Buildings. There was now a walkway next to the river and I no longer had to walk amidst the brush. As I walked on the path, I realized it lacked the connection to nature that walking on the earth provided.

I stopped walking when I reached my destination—the point where the Red and the Assiniboine met. It always fascinated me. Two waterways meeting, parting, flowing. Each was strong in its own right; each carried people and creatures great distances. Yet they co-existed without destroying each other. I watched in quiet satisfaction of Nature's eternal calm.

The sun began to set before I decided to return. I knew Nagam would be calmer by now. She always found a way to bring balance to chaos. She was the only thing keeping me together. I was still numb from them taking my children, but something within me kept me from falling apart as long as I knew she was there. I would feel her hand against me and I knew that everything would be OK.

I walked in silence, nodding occasionally to people I recognized, but never stopping. I followed the roads, taking the shortest route. I walked up Broadway and then went north on Sherbrook. My body always felt better after a walk like this.

The lights to our home were off and I assumed Nagam was asleep. I tried to move as quietly as possible, but the screen door always made a metallic screeching sound. I didn't hear her stir, so I took off my shoes and found some leftovers to eat. I made a coffee and ate hungrily. I didn't realize how hungry I was until the first piece of chicken was eaten. Then, the hunger demanded bread and coffee and whatever else I could find. When I was finished, my belly was full and I sat back. My situation was bleak. It was as terrible as I could imagine, yet I counted my blessings because of Nagam. She made it all bearable.

I didn't want to disturb her sleep, so I went outside to watch the world go to sleep. I took my cigarettes and sat down heavily in my chair on the porch. It was made of cedar and leaned back. It wasn't long before I fell asleep in it.

Protecting the Children

C hild Services showed up the day after Nagam's funeral.

"Migizi, I am very sorry for your loss," the same woman said. There was a much bigger man in a uniform next to her. Like the one before him, he didn't speak.

"If you were sorry, you'd let my children come home. Or at least visit me during the funeral." My grief was overwhelming and it competed with my anger to hurt these people. It took everything I could do to calm myself.

"As our report states, we are alarmed at the unstable nature of your home. Your wife's suicide reinforces that view."

"She was in shock because you took our children. She was tired. She took a few too many sleeping pills. It was an accident."

The woman looked coldly at me, her neck betraying the red blotches of stress. I met her stare, then looked away. If she wanted to be rude, that was her problem. I wasn't like that.

"The doctors confirm that she took an overdose. They confirm that it could not have been an accident. I can only go by what they say."

"So I'm lying?"

"We didn't say that, Migizi." The large man took a half step towards me. I don't think he realized that I was trained to kill with my bare hands. I sized him up and dismissed him in my mind.

"I want to see my children. When can I see my children?"

The woman paused. "We'll need to see. With the recent developments, I can't guarantee anything."

"You mean to say that I'll never see my children?" I could feel my neck strain against the tie I wore.

"I think we should take things one step at a time. We'll review your file at the appropriate time and see if things warrant a new approach." She spoke the words but no emotion crossed her face. I knew she was lying.

"You're not going to give my children back, are you? Who the hell do you think you are? We were a perfectly happy family until you came along. I own my home, have a job, and served in the army. I have medals to prove it."

"I know about your military career. It is very impressive and has counted a lot in your favour."

"Then let me have my children."

"We can only do what is best for the children. Their safety is our paramount concern. You must understand that we have a court-sanctioned duty of care to protect your children."

"Then you'll see that it's best for them to be with me."

"Your family is in crisis. Your first wife killed herself. Your second wife killed herself. You have a history of unexplained deaths in your family, including your grandchildren."

"They were in school. Under your care."

"Not under my care. I'm here in Winnipeg. Your children were hundreds of miles away."

"You know what I mean," I said. I began trembling and knew I had to get away from them or else I might do or say something I would regret. I left them standing in my kitchen and heard the screen door crash shut behind me. I needed to walk.

I walked north on Sherbrook until I came to Notre Dame. I turned left, westwards, and continued to walk. The cars and smells of the city began to overwhelm me and I turned north again onto Arlington. I could hear the crows but not my raven.

My eyelids were pulsating with the beating of my heart. I could swear I could hear the drums again. The Chief said they were the heartbeat of the earth. I began to twitch as my clothing irritated me. I took off my tie and threw it into someone's rosebushes. I regretted it, but I needed to take it off and I didn't want to carry it.

Arlington was full of homes built after the war. It was one of those streets that connected other streets. It wasn't like Sherbrook or Inkster Boulevard or a street that was alive with young families. Houses faced away from Arlington, onto the connecting roads. Arlington was for offices or shops or industrial buildings. I only knew Arlington for the bridge that went over the train yard below. It was controversial when it was bought, but I only knew this from gossip. I couldn't care less.

I walked to ease my pain. The only person capable of calming the rage inside me was no longer with me. She had passed into the other world.

The street became blurry to me and all I could focus on was the concrete below my feet. Houses disappeared and all I could see were the cold brick and steel buildings that housed car repair shops, printing presses and offices. I'm sure there were many more businesses, but those are the ones I recognized. I reached Logan and I looked left and right, not sure which direction to go.

I saw the bridge in front of me and knew I had no business crossing it. I could walk peacefully on Logan and then cut back towards the rivers and find peace next to the water. I should seek out the birch and the raven. Instead, I crossed the street and began to walk across the bridge.

It had a long approach and it took a while before I was actually on the bridge. I remembered the rumours. It was supposed have been built to cross the Nile in Egypt but got bought by Winnipeg instead. I didn't know if this was true. It was built by some firm in England. I doubt anything I hear as rumours. That being said, I no longer believed anything told to me as truth by the newspapers or government.

It looked temporary. It was all metal latched together in some geometric design that probably made it stronger. It looked like the types of bridges the army built as a temporary crossing during the war. But this one was much longer than anything I had seen over there. Below it was the history of

Winnipeg and of Canada: steel veins that ran from the eastern-most parts of Canada to the western-most parts. It was the railway that drove the push westwards through our people's lands. It was the railway and the push for settlers that inspired politicians to contain us in reserves and strip us of all humanity. No one would say it today and there is probably no evidence to support such a claim, but I believed it. It was the reason Louis Riel fought the government. It was the reason the government created the pass system on the reserves—to control and regulate the movement of our warriors.

I looked down at the rusted boxcars and oil containers. It looked like it had a hundred railway tracks with linked-up trains on some and rotting stock on others. I didn't know what they called a place like this. A depot or handling spot? It was as foreign to me as the reasoning of that stupid Child Services woman.

I walked mid-way across the bridge when I noticed a glossy black train locomotive making its way slowly down one of the tracks. It must be dropping off or picking up some stock. I thought of the way Myeengun played with his little toys. I knew I would buy him a train set when he was old enough.

I looked at the real thing below me and wondered at the money and power its owners wielded.

I became aware of the chain-link fence that extended from the side of the bridge up and over me. I guess they didn't want people to jump from the bridge. The idea never entered into my mind.

Before.

I looked below and then above. The fence would stop anyone who wanted to jump. Or, at least, anyone who hadn't done what I had. I jumped and clawed my way up the fence, hanging by my fingers as it crossed above me. It wasn't difficult at all compared to what we did at Monte la Difensa in Italy. And, then, they were shooting at us.

I reached the edge of the fencing and put my feet on the cross-bracing of the steel girders. I then walked up the steep girding, using the top metal bar of the fencing as a support. It took me less than a minute to be sitting on top of the fence that encased most pedestrians.

"I'm not most pedestrians," I said to myself.

I could feel that the air was different. I was only fifteen feet higher than when I was walking below, but it felt different. It was clearer and I noticed things without the interference of the fence. Even the trains looked different. They were in sharp focus. I looked up and saw an eagle in flight, circling high above me. I heard a *'kraa'* and turned to see if my raven had found me. I didn't see anything. I looked above at the eagle and couldn't find it any longer.

"You are stronger than this," came the voice. It was a boy's voice. I knew that voice.

"Geezis?"

"Hold on, my friend. Climb down." The raven was kraa'ing at me, but all I heard was the voice. My old friend; the innocence that had been violently torn from me the moment he stepped off that ledge.

"But you didn't."

"I was a child. You are a man."

"Nothing has changed."

"Nothing and everything has changed," he said.

"I have nothing left."

"You have three children who need you. They have already lost their mother and children of their own."

"I am lost. I don't belong."

"You belong with your people."

"My people are dead."

"Your people live so long as you live."

"I want to believe you but I am really talking to myself," I said out loud.

MIGIZI

I shook my head and looked at the sun. I looked down at the moving locomotive. I looked at the raven. I took my final step.

ABOUT THE AUTHORS

Baron Alexander was born in Winnipeg, Canada
He currently lives near London, England

Lucky Deschauer was born in Winnipeg, Canada
He currently lives in Dauphin, Manitoba

BARON ALEXANDER

If you'd like to follow Baron and receive free samples of his future writing before it is published, please visit www.baronalexanderbooks.com

Full, unabridged links to the Truth and Reconciliation Reports can be found on:
https://baronalexanderbooks.com/truth-and-reconciliation

Epilogue

A Story Based on the Truth

Hello! Aniin ~ Tân'si ~ Edlánet'é ~ Dahneh
Dha' ~
Nezu dágóts'e ~ Masì ~ Ah ~ Oki ~ Aba
Washded ~
Tawnshi ~ Wa-é ák-wé ~ Bonjour

Canada is the consequence of European colonial
enterprise. Its Indigenous peoples were essential for
the European powers in navigating, establishing trade
routes, and winning battles. When peace ensued
between London and Paris, the Indigenous peoples
became an inconvenience. Treaties were signed with
the Indigenous nations, and Canada eventually took
on the role as 'parent' for all Indigenous peoples
within its borders. No ownership was ever transferred
to the Indigenous nations of the land on which they
were to live.

The government of Canada decided to begin a
systematic assimilation of the Indigenous people with
the stated objective of 'taking the Indian out of the

Indian'. Residential schools were thought to be the most effective way of washing away the unwanted cultures, languages, and customs. Children were taken from their families and placed in schools (for many, year-round). They were not allowed to speak their language, act 'like Indians' or even wear their familiar clothing. (Despite knowing they hadn't reached India, Europeans continued to call Indigenous peoples Indians. Canadian legislation forces the continued use of this pejorative word by virtue of the *Indian Act*.)

The government of Canada recently admitted to practicing a culturally genocidal policy towards its Indigenous peoples as part of the Truth and Reconciliation process. Canadian residential schools forced children aged six (and some as young as four) to sixteen to work half a day in agricultural, domestic or service pursuits that would not put them in competition with settler occupations and professions. The other half-day was to be in class, learning to read, write, and speak English or French in order to assimilate them into Canadian society. Officially, over three thousand children died while in these schools. Unofficially, some put this figure closer to eighty thousand children. Historians will need to sift through the data before a definitive number is arrived at. For the most part, these children were buried without ceremony or headstone. Without birth certificates, their deaths went unrecorded and became lost to history. For parents, the consequence was the same—their child(ren) never came home.

MIGIZI

Those who overcame the scars of these schools, from 1876 to 1996, faced the institutional racism and prejudice of a country uninterested in their problems.

This story is an amalgam of real life stories and fiction. The truth lies within.

Baron and Lucky Deschauer
Dauphin, Manitoba, Canada, 2017

Timeline

1857   *Gradual Civilization Act* – Precursor to
        federally-funded residential schools. Purpose
        was to assimilate the Indigenous peoples of
        Canada.

1867   Dominion of Canada created by British
        Parliament, effective July 1, through *The
        British North America Act, 1867*. Provinces
        of New Brunswick, Nova Scotia, and the
        Province of Canada (which became Ontario
        and Quebec) became a country.

        The new country was to be called Canada.
        The name was originally the Saint-Lawrence
        Iroquoian word *Kanata*, meaning
        'settlement', 'village', or 'land'. The Saint-
        Lawrence Iroquoians are now extinct.

1869   *Gradual Enfranchisement Act* – Precursor to
        residential schools.

1869   Red River Rebellion, led by Louis Riel.
       Métis wanted independence.

1871   Province of Manitoba created.

       Rupert's Land and Northwest Territories
       incorporated into Canada.

       Provinces of Ontario and Quebec increased
       in size to include area near Hudson Bay.

       British Columbia joined Canada.

1879   Davin Report ("Report on Industrial Schools
       for Indians and Half Breeds", by Nicholas
       Flood Davin) submitted to Parliament. Led
       to federal funding of the residential school
       system. Schools were to be run and
       administered by churches.

1885   North-West Rebellion, led by Louis Riel.
       Rebellions such as these led to the adoption
       of the 'pass system' where Indigenous
       peoples required written permission to leave
       their reserves. There was no free movement
       if you were a member of a First Nation.

1894   *Indian Act* amended to make attendance of
       residential schools mandatory for all
       Indigenous children between seven and
       sixteen years old.

1905   Saskatchewan and Alberta joined Canada.

1907   Government of Canada chief medical officer and medical inspector for the Department of the Interior and Indian Affairs, Dr. Peter Bryce, reports that, in some residential schools, between six and twelve per cent of students died every year. This report focussed on the year 1907, with Dr. Bryce visiting thirty-five residential schools in person and administering a survey to others.

1908   *Indian Act* amended to make attendance mandatory for children between six and fifteen years old.

1922   After being forced out of the Public Service and his funding suspended, Dr. Bryce published a follow-up book: "The Story of a National Crime: An Appeal for Justice to the Indians of Canada", which showed that the government had done nothing to improve conditions following his 1907 report.

1945   *Family Allowance Act* required school-aged children to be enrolled in [residential] schools if parents were to receive money for their child.

1948   Compulsory attendance of residential schools ended. However, many Indigenous people continued to send their children to school or else they would be penalized financially.

1969   Department of Indian Affairs took sole
        control of the residential school system.

》   1980s TO 2016 **RECONCILIATION** 《

1993   Anglican Church of Canada apologizes for
        its role in the residential school system.

1994   Presbyterian Church of Canada recognizes
        its role in the residential school system and
        asks forgiveness.

1996   Last of the Indian Residential Schools in
        Canada closes, in Punnichy, Saskatchewan.

1998   United Church of Canada apologizes for its
        role in the residential school system.

2001   *The Truth Commission into Genocide in
        Canada* report, published.

2004   The Royal Canadian Mounted Police
        apologize for its role in the residential
        schools.

2008   Prime Minister of Canada, Stephen Harper,
        issues a formal apology for the creation of
        the residential school system and the abuses
        carried out within it.

2009   Pope "offered his sympathy and prayerful solidarity" to a delegation from the Assembly of First Nations for the Catholic Church's role and abuses in the residential schools.

2011   President of the University of Manitoba apologizes for its role in educating people who operated within the residential schools.

2015   Premiers of Manitoba, Saskatchewan, and Alberta apologize for their provinces' roles in the residential school system.

2015   Supreme Court Chief Justice Beverly McLachlin states in a May lecture to the Global Centre for Pluralism that Canada attempted to commit "cultural genocide" against Indigenous Canadians.

2015   *Truth and Reconciliation Commission* report published in June.

        Call to Action 58: "We call upon the Pope to issue an apology to Survivors, their families, and communities for the Roman Catholic Church's role in the spiritual, cultural, emotional, physical, and sexual abuse of First Nations, Inuit, and Métis children in Catholic-run residential schools.

2016   Premier of Ontario apologizes for Ontario's role in the residential school systems.

2022   Pope Francis apologizes to the First Nations, Metis, and Inuit people saying, "…with shame and unambiguously, I humbly beg forgiveness for the evil committed by so many Christians against the indigenous people."

Copyright © 2022 by Baron Alexander.

All rights reserved. No part of this publication may be reproduced, distributed or transmitted in any form or by any means, including photocopying, recording, or other electronic or mechanical methods, without the prior written per-mission of the publisher, except in the case of brief quotations embodied in critical reviews and certain other noncommercial uses permitted by copyright law. For permission requests, write to the publisher, addressed "Attention: Permissions Coordinator," at the address below.

Wilderwick Press, c/o Baron Alexander
Unit 4 Ashdown Court, Lewes Road, Forest Row
East Sussex, RH18 5EZ, United Kingdom

Or by email at baron@baronalexanderbooks.com

www.baronalexanderbooks.com

Publisher's Note: This is a work of fiction. Names, characters, places, and incidents are a product of the author's imagination. Locales and public names are sometimes used for atmospheric purposes. Any resemblance to actual people, living or dead, or to businesses, companies, events, institutions, or locales is completely coincidental.

Ordering Information: Special discounts are available on quantity purchases by corporations, associations, and others. For details, contact the publisher at the address above.

Wilderwick Press / Baron Alexander – First Edition

CPSIA information can be obtained
at www.ICGtesting.com
Printed in the USA
BVHW071441021222
653300BV00005B/591